Corsets and Codpieces

This book is dedicated to my fashion-loving granddaughter, Emma Elizabeth

Corsets and Codpieces

A History of Outrageous Fashion, from Roman Times to the Modern Era

By Karen Bowman

Skyhorse Publishing

Skyhorse Publishing books may be purchased in bulk at special discounts for
sales promotion, corporate gifts, fund-raising, or educational purposes. Special
editions can also be created to specifications. For details, contact the Special
Sales Department, Skyhorse Publishing, 307 West 36th Street, 11th Floor, New
York, NY 10018 or info@skyhorsepublishing.com.

Skyhorse® and Skyhorse Publishing® are registered trademarks of Skyhorse
Publishing, Inc.®, a Delaware corporation.

Visit our website at www.skyhorsepublishing.com.

10 9 8 7 6 5 4 3 2 1

Library of Congress Cataloging-in-Publication Data is available on file.

Cover design: Domenic Allen
Cover illustration credit: Karen Bowman

Print ISBN: 978-1-5107-0857-0
Ebook ISBN: 978-1-5107-0869-3

Printed in China

Contents

Author's Note

It is not possible in a book of this size to catalogue every twist and turn of fashion over 2 millennia, and so *Corsets and Codpieces* encapsulates those trends that era by era both elegantly and outrageously put their stamp upon the past. A social history of costume, it hopes to convey both the pride and the prejudices towards some of the more memorable aspects of clothing, giving you, the reader, a glimpse into what it was like to both wear the clothes as well as witness the attitudes and opinions of the times. Based on both primary sources and contemporary accounts, it promises to make entertaining and at times outrageous reading.

Karen Bowman

Introduction

Should we ladies or gents ever be transported back in time how thrilling it would be to wear the clothes of the time, except it would take an age just learning how to wear them. Until the early twentieth century a man's shirt was no more than an undergarment and so no self-respecting fellow would *ever* have appeared in his shirtsleeves, particularly in front of a lady. So used to freedom of movement, we would undoubtedly stumble over the hems of our skirts, struggle to breathe in a corset and fail to master all the languages of the fan. Being a woman in the past was a full-time occupation. We had to learn from childhood how to move in a long skirt: get used to taking little steps and only stride out perhaps when privately taking the air. We had to remember to *slew* ourselves sideways through a door in our crinolines and walk slightly in front of or behind a companion as it was impossible in such a monstrosity to get too close to anyone. Plus we had to remember to manoeuvre our bustles in such a way as to enable us to be able to sit down without there being a catastrophe.

To lift a skirt was an art, only really needing to be practised when mounting stairs if a girl had correctly learned the art at her mother's knee. She also learned how to gently let her foot push her skirt forward in front of her at the end of every step, thus never becoming entangled in fabric, but also remembering never to let her whole foot show. Turning was done with a single clean movement. In the case of farthingales, eighteenth-century hoops and later crinolines a lady's hands were always clasped in front of her or allowed to rest on the swell of the skirt, enabling her to control it. A woman's movement in such garments was always smooth as the slightest unguarded hip movement could set the whole inflated ensemble swinging in all directions!

The woman of yesterday was, just as today, a product of her clothes. During many periods, women had to appear carefree while in the vice-like grip of a corset plus walk smoothly from the knee, as the swaying of hips was considered indecent. In short, a girl had to *glide* with the effortless grace of a ghost …

With modern day knee-length skirts we have become accustomed to crossing our legs. This along with other modern habits are a world away from women sitting with their knees apart in order to create a 'broad lap', which when sitting would have given our clothes the recommended drape and the sitter poise. Crossing our arms correctly had to be learned. Rarely done when wearing a corset or hooped skirt, it was instead recommended to hold your arms out from your body, elbows bent helping to create an open space on either side of your torso thus drawing attention to your fashionably tiny waist. Arms were allowed to be crossed in the Regency era but only beneath the level of our 'short stays' so as not to spoil the line of our classically inspired gowns and long, willowy figures. This was to be the first time we women were not considered indecent in displaying our bare arms in public, even if it was usually only in the evenings.

What has remained unchanged is the fact that men and women whoever they were and whenever they lived have always communicated by the clothes they wear.

CHAPTER 1

Short Skirts, Long Beards

'We live not according to reason, but according to fashion'
Seneca, Roman philosopher, mid-first century AD

In matters of supremacy and conflict it is, as the saying goes, the one who 'wears the trousers' who usually has the upper hand. For centuries wearing 'braise' or britches has been a masculine prerogative affording the wearer vital ease of movement both in battle and physical work, something denied to women until emancipation in the early twentieth century. However, once in our history the opposite was true. When the Romans invaded our shores in the first century AD it was not only their weapons that won them this island. As every victory in history has relied as much on psychology as strategy there is no better illustration of mind over matter than the

Relief panel of the Great Ludovisi sarcophagus showing the battle scene between skirted Roman soldiers and a heathen enemy in trousers. From a tomb near the Porta Tiburtina, it dates from AD 250–60. *(Author's collection)*

Roman belief in himself. Thus, his armour atop his customary short tunic gave him, in his mind, that vital 'edge'.

The Roman way of life was totally alien to those living in the far-flung outposts of the Empire and the culture of the 'trouser-wearing' Britains spoke to the invader in volumes. 'Trousers' were the dress of heathens. As 'skirted' and 'clean cut', the Roman thought himself superior, a natural overlord whose rightful duty was to take our island from those they saw as subordinate. In reality, that idea that 'men in skirts' could actually have the decisive advantage is as unlikely today as it was then, but the Roman ethos of cleanliness in both body and dress elevated them in their own minds above the unclean, long-haired, bearded and trouser-wearing islanders. Once convinced, the Romans were nothing if not confident and as such pulled off one of the only two invasions of Britain.

This scenario is a perfect example of how 'clothes maketh man'; how they define him and how what you wear is as important as what you wield. Self- belief certainly elevated the Roman soldier, in his own mind at least, above his equally formidable foe. Diodorus Siculus, a Greek historian writing about the Celts of Gaul and Britain in the first century, described the Roman opponent as tall and 'terrifying' with 'rippling muscles under clear white skin. Their hair is blond, but not naturally so: they bleach it, to this day, artificially, washing it in lime and combing it back from their foreheads. They look like wood-demons, their hair thick and shaggy like a horse's mane.' Their costume he described as 'astonishing', adding that they wore 'brightly coloured and embroidered shirts, with trousers called braccae and cloaks fastened at the shoulder with a brooch', this latter garment heavy in winter, but light in summer. Striped or chequered in design, such cloaks had 'separate checks close together and in various colours', proving perhaps the Dark Ages were perhaps not so dark after all. Such were the British enemies of Rome dressed, with trousers available even to women. This was another reason the Romans shunned what they saw as female garb. In doing so it prevented them from wearing what they considered made them look 'more the heathen, than the elect'. Not about to surrender his native Mediterranean clothing even in the face of the freezing mists of Albion or snows of a Hibernian winter, the common soldier did have tried and trusted cold-weather clothing in the form of cloaks, socks, leg wrappings or bindings called puttees which wrapped from the ankle up to the calf, extra tunics and scarves which went some way to making life in this furthest outpost of the Roman Empire at least bearable. If not, supplies could be requested from Rome, as details from Tablet 255 of the Vindolanda Tablets, discovered in the 1970s and 1980s, disclose:

> Clodius Super to his Cerialis, greetings. I was pleased that our friend Valentinus on his return from Gaul has duly approved the clothing. Through him I greet you and ask that you send me the things which I need for the use of my boys, that is, six sagaciae, n saga, seven palliola, six [?] tunics, which you well know that I cannot properly get hold of here. May you fare well, my dearest lord and brother … To Flavius Cerialis, prefect, from Clodius Super, centurion

As the Romans assimilated into their new homeland eventually the braccae were worn by artillery soldiers in the coldest outposts but renamed 'femoralia', and were usually dark red and of varying lengths tied at the waist. Roman dignitaries, however, never stooped to wearing trousers and continued to wear the traditional toga over a tunic. Near the end of the Roman Empire the Emperor Honorius (d. 423 BC) prohibited men wearing 'barbarian' trousers in Rome, but insisted all Roman prisoners wear the heathen garment as a sign of their subjugation.

Keen to further establish themselves both in Rome and in Britain, the average Roman underlined his superiority by remaining clean-shaven, though beards were allowed to be worn by those of very high rank as a venerated mark of manhood. Across the Mediterranean the first shaving of a young man was done with the greatest ceremony and these 'first fruits of the chin' were carefully collected in a gold or silver box, in order to be afterwards presented to some God, as a tribute of youth. This recognition of manliness was something that carried through to later centuries, with the founder of the Holy Roman Empire, Otto the Great, allowed to *'swear by his beard'* on important matters, as well as the early Kings of France, for greater gravitas, including three hairs from their beard in the seals on their letters. Even England's Tudor chancellor, Thomas Moore, about to be executed on the scaffold, elevated his beard's importance in the eyes of those watching him. When laying his head on the block he moved it out of the path of the executioners axe apparently saying, 'My beard has not been guilty of treason; it would be an injustice to punish it.' It was this almost religious reverence for the beard that prompted the Romans to forbid the wearing of them by enemies, slaves or those deemed unworthy. This was to be the greatest cause of shame to a conquered people as the celts of Britain were nothing if not extremely hirsute.

With more than enough hair to spare, both the male and female Celt wore theirs long in multiple elaborate braids, sometimes with gold ornaments fastened to the end of them. A legendary tale tells of one woman having three braids of hair wound round her head, and the fourth hanging down her back to her ankles, though it is more likely to be folklore than fact. However, for a people that embraced an abundance of hair as outward signs of both masculinity and femininity to have their chins shaved and their hair shorn was the greatest affront and disgrace a heathen could receive. For the Romans it was the perfect way by which to subjugate their enemies. Not until women willingly cut theirs as a symbol of emancipation did hair became less status symbol and more fashion statement. But that was going to take upward of a thousand years and before that the Romans would have long left our shores and the British provinces reduced to Saxon rule.

Stepping into the void left by the Romans it was inevitable that the new Germanic overlords had their own rules and regulations for hair. Just as it had been for the preceding Celts, hair was a symbol of virility and strength. It was expressive. Framing the face it was easily visible and easily subject to change; it could be dyed, shaped or worn loose. Longer hair meant high birth and again like the Celts, denoted a free man. It was a visual and social badge of a warrior aristocracy. For the Saxons their hair was protected by law with penalties if the law was broken. It was forbidden to seize a man by the beard and tear any hairs from it or from his head. By the laws of King Alfred it was against the law to cut off a man's beard and if such happened he was entitled to 20 shillings compensation. If a long-haired boy had his hair cut without his parent's consent, the wrongdoer would be in receipt of a very heavy fine. The same applied for cutting the hair of a freewoman. Even to snatch a head-covering from her head was an offence.

With British Christianity still in its infancy in the eighth century, the Venerable Bede spoke of a man's beard 'as a mark of the male sex and of age, and is customarily put as an indication of virtue'. However, on Ash Wednesday 1094, when the religion had taken a deeper hold, Archbishop Anselm of Canterbury refused to give his blessing to men who 'grew their hair like girls'. At Rouen two years later, a church council decreed that no man should grow his hair long but have it cut as a Christian. Just prior to William of Normandy's invasion of Britain thirty years earlier, the Saxon King Harold sent spies into France as – should an invasion take place – he wished to know what a Frenchman looked like in order to distinguish them from his own men on the battlefield. On their return the spies reported back that all the Norman soldiers were 'surely priests as each had their entire faces, plus both lips shaved', this at a time when it was customary for the English to leave their own upper lips 'uncut'. Such observations are indeed borne out by the Bayeux Tapestry, an embroidered record of the subsequent invasion, as it shows the English with moustaches and long hair; the Normans are short-haired and clean-shaven.

Facial hair was also an issue with men of holy persuasion. The Benedictine monk Orderic Vitalis (1075–1142), who was reputed to be an honest and trustworthy chronicler of his times,

The beard was a sign of veneration in many cultures and to remove it forcibly was a punishable offence. Detail of a miniature of Dagobert cutting his tutor's beard, from the *Grandes Chroniques de France*, France (Paris), 1332–50. *(British Library digitised manuscripts)*

when referring to the court of William Rufus (1087–1100), the third son of William I, wrote that a man's long hair suggested dubious morals and made him crazy and prone to 'revel in filthy lusts'. Bishop Ernulf of Rochester (1114–24) detested how some men with long beards ignored the fact that they inadvertently dipped them into their drinking cups, while an earlier bishop, observing how some hermits and holy men did not shave or cut their hair, made the derogatory remark that 'If a beard makes a saint, nothing is more saintly than a goat'. William of Malmesbury, being particularly scathing about aristocrats with long hair, cited it as a sign of homosexuality and decadence. He even blamed the English defeat at the Battle of Hastings on it as he said it led men who should have defended their kingdom with much more vigour to behave no better than women.

But whatever went on about a man's chin the clothes on his back were not as easy to come by. Whereas today we easily buy clothing and our recent ancestors were at least able to obtain the ready-made fabrics by which to make them, earlier in history it was case of having to cultivate sheep, the source of your clothing in the first place. Anglo-Saxon and early medieval clothing was woven out of linen or wool, with the earliest sheep being mostly brown and grey. After sheep were domesticated, more native white sheep were bred in order to produce more white wool which was thought easier to dye. British wool was far superior to that of other countries, due to the cool, wet climate and longer grazing season. This in turn produced long fibres which resulted

An Iron Age loom. (© Sue Walker White)

in a finer, stronger thread. Wool was then shorn from the sheep, sorted, scoured, combed or carded and then spun, usually using a drop spindle. Once spun into thread it was woven more often than not on a warp-weighted loom. Such looms were the mainstay of all fabric production and produced anything from simple cloths to intricate tapestry work. Looms also varied in width with some able to make fabrics almost 2m wide with the weaver walking back and forth while weaving, alternatively two or three women would sit side by side and pass the shuttles forwards and backwards between themselves. Card weaving (or tablet weaving) was used to make belts, trim and fringes. Anglo-Saxon and Viking crafts also included a netting technique called sprang, which like an early form of knitting was used to produce caps, bags and stockings.

Once woven the fabrics were sewn into clothing using woollen thread and with needles originally made of bronze but later of steel. Needles themselves were extremely valuable, varying in worth from a yearling calf for a common needle to an ounce of silver for an embroidery needle. Just like today, all seams were on the inside of the garment except for those made of leather which were sewn on the outside for better weatherproofing. Double-layered winter cloaks were constructed of heavy wool, the outside also weatherproofed by oiling. Inside, as lining, there was usually a layer of smooth linen of a bright, single colour laying to rest the misconception that all Dark Age and Early English clothing was dull and drab.

A mastery over the art of dying meant that up until and beyond the High Middle Ages English men and women were clothed in colours of almost every hue. Well-practised but not always fully understood, it was both revered and treated with suspicion, especially on the domestic front. For many it was considered a strange and magical process, with rules about which days of the week or month were proper dyeing days, with dyers also having a reputation for being herbal healers, since many dyestuffs were also used in folk medicine. Ultimately, dyeing was considered a woman's craft, there being an air of taboo about carrying out the 'alchemistic' practice in the presence of men. In an ancient Irish text called the *Book of Lismore* a passage recounts the moment when St Ciaran's mother tells him to go out of the house, since it was unlucky to have men in the house while dyeing cloth. In a fit of pique he left but not without cursing the cloth so that it dyed unevenly.

One ancient word for dyestuffs is 'ruaman'; the word 'ruam' meaning red, a colour obtained from the madder plant, indicating that most dyes were sourced from plants, roots and vegetables. Yet no fibres, thread or fabric would keep its depth of colour if not 'fixed'. This was done with a 'mordent', a French word meaning 'to bite', which helped the dyes penetrate the fibres instead of simply lying on the top and being easily washed off.

Varied and interesting, mordents were naturally occurring and when mixed with the dye not only stopped colours fading over time but also added to their depth. Popular mordents were iron, which could be obtained from ore and was known to 'sadden' colours or make then greyer, as did oak-galls, otherwise growths on plants. Copper, or the bluish-green patina formed on copper by oxidation and known as verdigris, was common, as well as alum, a sulphate obtained from wood ash, chips of oak or alder wood. In order to fix and 'brighten' colours the favourites were burnt seaweed or kelp and lastly urine, which was readily available and collected by women in the mornings and left to grow stale to increase its strength and potency.

Colours themselves were taken from the roots, leaves, flowers or bark of plants with different parts of the same plant often yielding different hues. Lichens were a favourite as they produced 'fast' permanent dyes and if gathered in July and August and dried in the sun, could then be fermented with stale urine, sometimes for as long as three weeks over low heat, to dye wool in an iron dye-pot. Yellow, with a mordent of alum, could be obtained from the barks of birch, ash and crab-apple trees. Wood and leaves of the poplar, the young roots of bracken, bramble and broom, onion skins, nettles, moss and marigold were just as effective in creating yellow, as were heather, dogwood and common dock leaves. Teasel, water pepper and the flower heads of

St John's wort, if soaked in ammonia (urine) for several days, did the same. A plant called weld yielded a light, clear yellow, as did meadowsweet sorrel, gorse blossoms and mare's tail.

Until 1498, when Vasco da Gama opened a trade route from India to Europe to import indigo, blue was commonly produced by fermenting woad leaves. Blackthorn, privet and elderberries could also be used, while bilberries and the roots of the yellow iris if fixed with iron also produced blue. Mud boiled in an iron pot would produce a very colourfast dull, black dye, the mixture able to produce a glossy black if oak chips or twigs were added. Brown could be obtained by using birch, bog-bean, briar and bramble roots. Dulse, otherwise known as seaweed, also produced various shades of brown, as did hops, larch needles, speedwell and lichens mixed with iron in a dye-pot. If green was required then foxgloves, flowering rush, the crumpled buds and leaf fronds of bracken, horsetail, nettles and privet berries would work. If a really dark green was desired then mixing weld with sheep dung gave a good depth of colour not to mention smell. Pinks and reds were derived from madder roots and a dyer could produce a whole spectrum of shades from coral to rust by skilfully raising the temperature of the dye vat by a few degrees. Blackthorn in a mordent of alum produced orange. Lady's bedstraw and cudbear lichen mixed with ammonia was the means of getting crimson.

The most highly valued, and noblest, colour of ancient times was purple. Like other colours, various shades could be produced from plant dyes such as dandelion, deadly nightshade, spindle, the flower heads of St John's wort and the berries and bark of the blackthorn. However, the strongest shade of purple was derived by using molluscs such as murex.

Purple was first produced in or near the city of Tyre in Lebanon during the Roman period. According to Pliny the Elder's book *Historia Naturalis,* the process was a long and laborious business involving whelk mucus, honey, salt and water, and long-term heating in a lead vessel. Those who invested their time and effort in its manufacture came to be known as 'purple-makers'. Probably the worst aspect of the job was the smell. The tiny shellfish first had to be crushed down (on average 1,000 shellfish would yield enough dye for colouring one cloak) then put into water. After ten days fermenting the liquid was full of pigment and wood ash was added for alkali, then the whole stinking concoction was left again to rot down, well covered to keep out light. This was essential as light would strip out the red in the liquid and resulted in the dyer being left with a pot of 'blue' not 'purple'. At the end of a prescribed time there was no other way of ascertaining if the light blue dye you had was ready than first to feel it to test its alkalinity (smooth if done, rough if not) then, if still unsure, to taste it. Once satisfied a strip of cloth or linen was soaked in the dye for half an hour after which it was taken out and exposed to the air. It is at this point, finally, at the end of the long and smelly process that a chemical reaction took place and the material, at first still white, after a few minutes changed to a watery green before transforming to the deep and vibrant colour purple so sought after.

CHAPTER 2

Modest Medieval

'There's never a new fashion but it's old.'

Geoffrey Chaucer

'Clothes maketh the man', or so the saying goes, and the High Middle Ages (*c.* 1000–1200) is generally accepted as the time when clothing first began to evolve into what we think of today as fashion. It was no longer the purpose of fabrics solely to cover nakedness, as it was for our Stone Age and Dark Age cousins. With technology fronting changes such as the spinning wheel, which replaced the hand-held distaff, and the horizontal loom which simplified textile production, clothing became a conscious choice of cut of shape and so style became a deliberate symbol of status. How we dressed became a means of differentiating between social classes and prompted displays of individualism. But to those in powerful places, individualism was divisive and could lead to social and civil unrest. Constantly afraid of 'self-expression' and 'individuality', the Church thought it could cure the people of the sins of vanity, greed and licentiousness by regulating who was allowed to wear what, where, when and how. It was not always easy in the face of new colours and fabrics being brought back from the crusades but with rules and punishments for those that transgressed, some modicum of order was achieved.

So with the advent of 'fashion' came inevitable clothing censorship, and for centuries to come laws would try to contain it while men and women would go to outrageous lengths to re-invent it. Not wanting to be left out, the Church would try – and in many respects succeed – in taking control of it. With the overriding impression of Middle-Age clothing being one of modesty, it is fair to say that women especially were never again to experience quite such pressure to be 'overdressed' from neck to toe until the Victorian age. In both eras, it was modesty by Church decree!

With only a minimum of flesh allowed to be on display, the medieval woman turned her attention to exactly how she could individualise her costume. Dressing from the inside out first, she would have worn 'brais', a medieval form of underwear consisting of a pair of separate loose stockings or hose fastened at the waist by a cord. These were made of linen and more often than not of different colours. The first full-length garment was then the shift or chemise, again made of linen covered over by a gown usually of wool called a kirtle or a cotehardie. Laces proved to be a medieval girl's best friend, as once threaded and pulled they contoured otherwise shapeless gowns into a showcase for the curves of breast, hip and thigh. Buttons (stemming from the French *bouton* for bud or *bouter* to push) were available but usually only to adorn clothing, and it would be a long time before the humble button would reach its indispensable usefulness and the overriding reason for this was its counterpart the 'buttonhole'. A necessary 'opening', it was vehemently frowned upon as flesh, no matter how small a glimpse, could be seen through it when a button was used.

A noblewoman of the fourteenth century wearing a variation of the cotehardie, the scandalous side-less surcote. This garment was condemned by the Church as the curve of a woman's waist could be seen within and so it was considered a temptation. It was referred to as 'Hell's Windows'. *(Author's collection)*

Should our medieval lady have had the money to alternate her outer garments then she may also have chosen to fly in the face of the Church and don the abominable side-less surcoat, possibly the most scandalous piece of clothing at the time. A variation of the cotehardie, it was wickedly open at the sides from shoulder to hip. Introduced late in the thirteenth century, this style became popular by the second half of the fourteenth century, its deep armholes allowing men to feast their eyes on the shape of a woman's body beneath. Such an indecent invitation was deemed so immoral in the eyes of the Church that clergy dubbed the garment 'Hell's Windows' and condemned it from the pulpit.

Equally condemned from on high was a woman's headwear, hats at this time being universally worn. Pulling off anyone's hat was considered a crime, while forcibly removing a woman's headdress was to accuse her of being a harlot. Depending on one's rank, occupation and the time of the year, hats could vary from linen head-warmers, straw or felt hats, mesh coifs, 'sallet' helmets (from which it is alleged we get the word 'salute' due to the hand movement required to raise the visor on a helmet to expose one's face and so affirm your identity) to mitres and crowns. The most recognisable headwear of the Middle Ages was large, ornate, sculptured and extremely high.

Between 1430 and 1440 width was the object of hat fashion but later in the century it was height. The most characteristic of this high fashion in headwear was the cornet or steeple, which rose to unique heights from the head. Originally a Continental style, the hennin originated in Burgundy and became one of the most distinctive forms of headwear worn in human history. Beginning simply as a stiff cone with the wide end sat on the crown of the head, the point jutted up and slightly back. Over time the cone got longer and longer, reaching upwards of 4ft, and keeping the steeple headdress on the head was no easy matter. At first it was pinned to a simple cloth cap that tied beneath the chin. But as the steeples grew taller, women developed more substantial under-caps with sturdy anchors. It has even been suggested in some texts that women resorted to glue, though this is unlikely, especially in England where a truncated form of the hennin was favoured over the dizzy heights of its Continental counterpart. To add to this ever upward illusion it became fashionable to show no hair beneath the steeple headdress, so women plucked their hair up to the line of the headdress.

A fantastical variation on this theme was the 'ram's horn' headdress, its name deriving from the two sculpted 'horns' that stuck out from either side of the temple. Again, these curved cones were constructed of wire mesh that was secured to a snug-fitting skullcap. Thin, gauzy veils could be hung from the ends or were draped between the horns, or they could be adorned with small ornaments. First seen in the late 1300s, they soon went out of fashion but both the ram's horn and steeple headdresses were still known as hennins.

These hennins, along with the other outrageous horned headdresses favoured by ladies, were the subject of much abuse from clerics and moralists. Pierre de Gros, a Franciscan theologian, in his treatise on theology, law and history, *Le Jardin des Nobles*, written in 1464, complained that 'the younger and more beautiful the ladies were, the higher were the chimneys that they carried!'. It was also a favourite pastime to demonise the fashion with one artist using the hennin to symbolise evil in his particular portrayal of the age-old subject of the Temptaion of St Anthony. The hennin, to his mind being both alluring and sinful, was worn by the temptress in his adaptaion of the theme, the wearing of a steeple hat and trailing veil initially suggesting nothing out of the ordinary. It is only when we discover that her feet have been drawn as tallons that it is clear the charming woman is really the Devil in disguise.

Ridicule did not stop at paintings and sculpture. Thomas Conecte apparently went as far as mounting a one-man crusade against what he considered a most extravagant headdress. A native of Brittany and a friar of the Carmelite order, he was well known and celebrated through parts of Flanders – modern-day Belgium – for his preachings. As his reputation proceeded him, when it was known he was about to visit a town the local inhabitants made provisions for him in their finest squares and erected large platforms complete with an altar. Here, beneath decorations of rich cloths and tapestries, he would say mass, attended by some monks of his order as well as his disciples, who had followed him on foot while he himself rode a small mule. A man who abhorred corruption, Thomas's sermons would blame the vices and sins of the individual, and

Christina of Pisa, born 1363, wears the horned headdress known as a divided hennin. From the *Court Magazine*, 1840. *(Author's collection)*

more especially those of the clergy who publicly kept mistresses, on humanity's failure to uphold vows of chastity either to God or within a marriage contract. Similarly, he blamed all ladies, noble or otherwise, 'who dressed their heads in so ridiculous a manner' and who wasted money on the luxuries of apparel. He was so vehement in his speeches that women dared not appear at his sermons in anything that would incite his condemnation, or cause him to 'excite little boys to torment and plague them', giving the lads as reward 'certain days of pardon' from their sins for carrying out his orders. Thomas found this arrangement quite satisfactory and ordered the boys to shout after such women, '*Au hennin, Au hennin!*' while they chased them down the street in an attempt to pull the offending headdresses from their heads. In such instances ladies were forced to seek any place of shelter available, as it was usual for undignified scuffles to ensue between those in pursuit and the servants and defenders of the ladies.

As a result of Thomas Conecte's abuse of noble ladies with high headdresses, many females refused to attend his sermons altogether, or if they did, to escape his attention, they wore the low caps of peasant women or nuns. But this reform was shortlived, for just as a snail draws in its horns when anyone passes by, once the vitriolic preacher had moved on to tyrannise another town his doctrines were forgotten and the colossal headdresses came out once again. This proved if little else that there is nothing like public ridicule to inspire change, even if it is only temporary!

On the other hand, the wimple, also spelled 'whimple', was a completely different story. Coming from a word meaning 'to flow in wavelets', it was a very modest head covering for women from as early as AD 500. It continued to be a mainstay of women's fashion up until the 1500s as it was customary for married women to cover their hair as a sign of modesty. Consisting of a length of

Hennins varied in shape and size, as seen in this *Woodcut Au Hennin Female Head-Dresses Fifteenth Century Midieval France* from 1877. *(Author's collection)*

soft cloth wrapped around the throat, it passed under the chin from one side of the head to the other and was pinned to the hair under a 'couvrechef', which covered the top of the head and flowed down over the shoulders. The wimple and veil combination was an excellent headdress for displaying respectability, and was greatly favoured by the Church since it covered everything except a woman's face and especially a woman's ears. Strange though it may seem, there was a train of thought at the time that believed that the Virgin Mary conceived the Christ child Jesus through her ears. No wonder the Church was worried. The wimple is still today the most recognised part of a nun's habit and still covers the ears. The wimple also covered the hair. Just as in Roman times, hair was a symbol of both status and sex and as the thickness and condition alluded to a woman's fertility, such a temptation was to be omitted from the view of all men except the husband or father of the woman in question. It was also useful for a woman to keep less than clean hair out of the way as open fires and general day-to-day town smells were not easily washed from hair that was often over 3ft long!

Of course, nuns had their hair shorn as a symbol of their renunciation of all worldly temptation and their fertility. Monks also had their hair cut and were clean-shaven as a symbol of servant-hood, and slavery, albeit slaves of Christ. The nun's habit totally covered the body, de-sexualising the woman underneath, but was not necessarily black, as we have come to believe. In medieval strict Orders women wore totally undyed woollen garments to proclaim their poverty and so their clothing would be a greyish white, sometimes even brown. Particularly devout orders would require a hair shirt to be worn underneath everything else.

The ordinary medieval woman was, however, a far more colourful character, literally. Even the humble peasant had colourful clothing. Dyes were common and came from different sources, some more expensive than others. By utilising plants, roots, lichen, tree bark, nuts, crushed insects, molluscs and iron oxide almost every colour of the rainbow could be achieved. New and exciting colours appeared in England by way of the crusades, such as carmine and lilac, as well as fabrics such as muslin, cotton, satin and damask.

Although blue woad had been daubed upon the faces and bodies of Dark Age warriors centuries before, the blue adopted by medieval French kings was indigo, made available to Europe by the Portuguese explorer Vasco da Gama who discovered a sea route to India in the fifteenth century. Importers could now avoid the heavy duties imposed by Greek and Persian middlemen and the lengthy and dangerous land routes which had previously been used. There were no gender assigned medieval colours, no pink for feminine or blue for masculine. It was in fact the reverse. Blue was associated with the Virgin Mary and conveyed gentleness. It was considered a weak colour in comparison to pink as pink came from red and red was the embodiment of power, passion, wealth and blood. White stood for purity, but was not worn by brides – whatever their station, people were simply married in the very best clothing they owned.

As with all fashion down the centuries, clothing had the power to communicate; the power to express, wealth, rank and power. Fabrics embodied social class. Perhaps more than male dress, female attire in the Middle Ages definitely indicated a woman's social status, and morality. In an effort to distinguish the honourable women from the prostitutes specific sumptuary laws were enforced.

While it was not required by law for medieval prostitutes to emulate their ancient Greek and Roman sisters by dressing deliberately seductively in short, flame-coloured togas, applying copious amounts of make-up, wearing sandals that spelled out 'follow – me' in the sand (earning them the name 'street walker') and dyeing their hair yellow to differentiate themselves from respectable women, yellow was a colour effectively assigned them. There is a theory that this directly mirrored the colour assigned to medieval Jews who were also viewed with suspicion and considered outcasts from medieval society.

To be specific, different places had different costume restrictions with Hamburg in Germany, for example, making its prostitutes wear red hats with enormous red wings at each side so they were easier to locate. In Austria it was a yellow cloth under their arm and in Switzerland a hat with yellow balls on it. Unlike her Roman sister, the medieval prostitute could not rise through the ranks to become a great courtesan and as such was restricted from wearing any type of luxury fabrics at all.

Fur was an interesting item of clothing in its own right. Once used mainly for warmth it was now principally for decoration and was possibly the foremost fabric that denoted status. Strict rules were designed to protect the hierarchy of those who were entitled to wear it. Sumptuary laws of 1337 first restricted the wearing of furs, with legislation of 1363 decreeing that women were, in general, to be dressed according to the position of their fathers or husbands. Sable, vair or squirrel fur, ermine, and miniver, the un-spotted white fur derived from the stoat, was to be confined to the ladies of knights with a rental above 200 marks a year. Going down the social scale things did not improve. Yeomen's wives were not to wear silk veils, while the wife or daughter of a knight-bachelor was not allowed velvet and females in the family of a labourer were not to wear clothes beyond a certain price or 'girdles garnished with silver'. Peasants were warned they should never wear more than one colour at once, except, perhaps, a different coloured hood for special occasions.

Whatever solitary colour a peasant was allowed to wear at any one time, dyed fabric faded quickly if not mixed with a mordant or fixing agent. The best and easiest to access was human urine, a substance collected daily for the purpose of fulling and dyeing cloth. Urine was best stale and so was left for a couple of weeks to decompose after which it produced a powerful ammonia which was used to remove the grease from fabrics and fix colours. Medieval craftsmen had recipe books for making dyes, some of the information having been passed down in Latin from ancient times, but many women would have some knowledge of basic dyes and would collect the family's morning urine – which was most effective – and store it until needed to help dye the wool.

Eastern England especially grew rich on the back of the country's wool. Notorious for its lack of naturally occurring stone, building materials were able to be bought in with wool proceeds to enable churches to be built to cathedral proportions with celestial vaulted roofs and flying buttresses. Wool was such a significant source of income to the English Crown in 1275 that the first ever export tax was imposed on its shipment abroad. It was called the 'Great Custom' and to ignore it was at one time punishable by the cutting off of a hand. Wool also originated the label 'spinster' from 'spin' as women made most of the clothes. The importance of wool to the English economy is still evident today as the presiding officer of the House of Lords sits upon an official chair stuffed with wool known as the 'Woolsack'.

Although most domestic clothes making was done from start to finish at home by females, surprisingly there was ready-made clothing available. At special times of the year clothing might be given to the poor by the wealthy as part of celebrations or as gifts from the Church or wealthy patrons who engaged in such acts both out of charity and for the sakes of their souls. A peasant woman who worked for a well-off family in town could expect to receive a new gown as part of her yearly upkeep. Not only was this a form of charity on the part of the employer, it also ensured that the staff they employed were reasonably dressed and fit to be seen as part of their retinue.

A townswoman had the choice of making her own well-fitting clothes or purchasing some items form a mercer, such as basic shifts, while making and decorating her outer garments herself. Mercers' shops also sold accessories, like gloves, caps, socks and hose. She could employ a tailor to make her an outfit or buy second-hand clothes from him that had been ordered by others but not paid for. A new owner of an existing item of clothing was at liberty to have it re-cut for a better fit or unpicked and remade inside out so that any faded outer faces would be replaced

A high-waisted costume with a truncated hennin, c. 1470. (Author's collection)

by fresher inner colours. Noblewomen's clothes and those of her family were always made by a tailor, though the lady would have an up-to-date knowledge of what was fashionable and how clothes were made. Once out of fashion a lady often handed down garments to her ladies-in-waiting, perhaps with trains trimmed and some ornamentation removed so as to befit the new wearer's status. As well as universally recycled, medieval clothing indicated class differences, and was used to mark religious, military and chivalric orders as well as single out pilgrims, Jews, muslims, heretics, lepers and prostitutes, the insane and individuals condemned to death.

Shoes and Codpieces – the Long and the Short of It …

We cannot, of course, leave the Middle Ages without mentioning two outrageous fashions which allude to the blatant citing of male sexuality, first male footwear and secondly the codpiece. As if not to be outdone by the fair sex, as ladies headwear ranged ever higher, so too men's footwear became ever longer. By 1367 a fashion for long-toed shoes called Krakows, after the capital city of Poland at that time, emerged and by 1450 the shoes were known as pikes or pigaches after a kind of pail with a long handle. A decade later they were universally recognised as Poulaines as in 'souliers a la Poulaine', otherwise shoes in the Polish fashion. The monstrosities lasted over 300 years, with the term Poulaine always referring to the long, pointed beak of the shoe only and not the shoe itself. The shoes were eventually legislated against as the ridiculous extensions became longer and longer until walking was almost impossible. Just as with women's headdresses, the Church was shocked at the extravagance of such footwear as well as its obvious sexual overtones. Blatantly phallic, young men tended to stuff wool and moss in the extensions to keep them erect and a popular vulgarity was to paint the extensions flesh-coloured. The Church were appalled at how a humble shoe could be elevated into something, which depending on a gentleman's rank, could extended to almost 24in longer than the foot and glorify masculine sexuality in such an obvious way.

The clergy supported legislation against the shoe exclaiming that it had incited God's rage and exacted his wrath against mankind in the shape of the great Black Plague of 1347, when almost half the population had died. They also condemned the fashion because they claimed by wearing such footwear men had been physically unable to pray, though in reality it was probably more in keeping with the way some young men laced their hose too tightly to their doublets that prevented them from kneeling. Whatever the reason, the shoes were branded both as Satan's Curse or Satan's Claw and university professors were banned from wearing them. Laws were brought in to regulate the shoes and during the reign of Edward III (1312–77) pointed toes were prohibited for all who did not have an income of at least £40 a year.

When it comes to the codpiece much has been said about it but almost nothing written. It was a fashion born out of necessity and in this period of history it was a simple covering to prevent a man's genitals from being exposed when the medieval tunic rose from knee-high in 1340 to thigh-high by the 1360s. It may have been the fashion but it was not a wise move, especially as the design of men's hosiery had not had a chance to catch up. Oblivious to this state of affairs, tunics, which should be thought of as doublets or modern-day jackets, eventually levelled out at hip height between 1420 and 1440. All was not totally lost as men did wear shirts beneath their doublets which tucked into the individual hose and were attached by laces to the doublet's hem and gave as much support and coverage a linen shirt could provide. Chaucer, well aware of the dilemma, gave these words to the parson in his *Canterbury Tales* to illustrate the state of affairs:

Alas! some of them show the very boss of the privy member and the horrible pushed-out testicles that look like the malady of hernia in the wrapping of their hose, and the buttocks

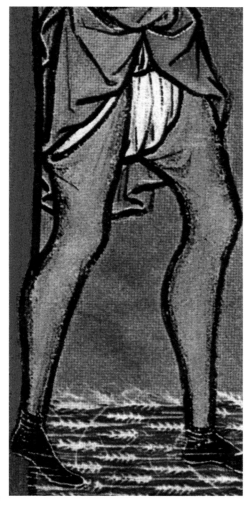

Medieval hose were fastened individually to a man's upper garment giving rise for the need for what was to become known as the codpiece. *(British Library digitised manuscripts)*

of such persons look like the hinder parts of a she-ape in the full of the moon. And moreover, the members that they show by the fantastic fashion of making one leg of their hose white and the other red, make it seem that they are corrupted by the fire of Saint Anthony, or by other such misfortune.

With men performing physical daily tasks glimpses of the male sexual organs became commonplace and a general outcry prompted Edward IV in 1482 to introduce legislation. The law, which forbade persons below the rank of lord to expose their private 'sinful' parts by wearing short doublets, was at first ignored as sewing the hose together would make necessary front access almost impossible. Later, the first three-cornered fabric codpieces – cod meaning 'scrotum' or 'bag' in Middle English – were tied or partially stitched over the gap in the front of the hose. The codpiece was to remain relatively unobtrusive during the Middle Ages but was to re-emerge as a major fashion accessory in the coming century, as the Tudors will illustrate in the next chapter.

No reference to 'the medieval' would be complete without the inclusion of armour, that steel casing a man wore exclusively to cover his body in time of conflict, turning him from mortal flesh into a living fortress. By no means a fashion statement, it nevertheless prompted a significant change in male/female clothing by taking men out of what could be described as the 'universal tunic' worn by both sexes, albeit with different cuts and embellishments. Now men needed to don 'underwear' beneath their plate armour in order to prevent their skin chafing and bruising and so garments such as aketons, gambesons and hacketons became available. Also known as 'Welsh Jacks', Scottish Jacks and 'doublets of fense', these tight-fitting, quilted coats were sewn and stuffed with linen or even grass to help absorb blows to the armour on the battlefield. One example of padding is the gambeson of Edward the Black Prince which consists of five layers: two linen shells and the wool stuffing in between, an inner satin lining and coat of arms in blue and red velvet applied to the front. From the twelfth century until at least the end of the fifteenth century they were also used by lower ranking soldiers whose wages did not stretch to full body armour.

The idea of a knight in shining armour was the product of Victorian romanticism but the numerous pieces of armour that made up a suit, which could weigh up to 27 kilos, did have to be kept clean and in full battle order. Squires rarely used water to clean the metal as that was wasteful, especially if out in the field. Instead, an abrasive was applied such as sand, where smaller pieces of armour were immersed in a barrel and rolled to enable the sand to remove mud and mire. Larger pieces were scoured with a cloth frequently dipped into sand mixed in with both vinegar and urine. Medieval mercenary Sir John Hawkwood rose to become commander of the famous White Company in 1364, his army known by that name for the scrupulously clean armour he demanded of his men.

Not for the first time would military clothing have a bearing on what later was to be worn in civilian life. Arming jackets coupled with the necessary knitted leggings or stockings gave men a new silhouette, pushing the male forward into garments that for centuries would become doublets and hose leaving them totally independent of women, who from this point on would continue the tradition of wearing skirts.

CHAPTER 3

Ruffs and Hose

'Alas, poor verdingales must lie in the streete,
To house them no doore in the citee made meete,
Syns at our narrow doores they in cannot win,
Send them to Oxforde, at Brodegates to get in.'

Poem by poet and translator John Heywood, 1560

It was the young 16-year-old Spanish Princess, Catherine of Aragon, who first introduced England to the vardingale. Wearing it in 1501, when she arrived in England to marry Prince Arthur Tudor, it would become the fashion for well over a century, going from a modest garment to the extravagant 'wheel and drum' farthingales favoured by her step-daughter Elizabeth I (1533–1603). No longer were dresses going to be allowed to hang free, as they had done in the medieval period with a woman's neckline the prime focus of attention. From the moment Catherine stepped ashore after her treacherous three-month journey from her old homeland to her new, the Englishwoman's dress was to be shaped and dramatically increased in size.

'Verdugadas', 'vertugale' and the 'verdingale' derives from the Spanish word 'verdugos', meaning 'smooth twigs put out by a tree that has been cut or pruned', and relates to the fact this new skirt was held away from the body by horizontal seams thread through with wood. Differing from later farthingales which became the stiffened petticoat that a woman's dress was draped over, this skirt, first seen in Spain in the late 1470s, was an outer garment, its cone shape achieved via hoops, called aros, gradually increasing in size from the waist to the hem.

Pedro Garcia de Benabarre painted the earliest image of this dress in 1470 as part of a larger work. The earliest references to this style of dress come from a courtier-historian by the name of Palencia, who, writing about Juana of Portugal, Queen of Castile, thought she wore the creation to hide a pregnancy. There is no proof of this, but the fashion spread like wildfire as it was copied by the Queen's ladies and adopted by Queen Isabel of Portugal. Isabella's confessor, Hernando de Talavera, a Spanish monk, was less than complimentary about this style of clothing and was not afraid to voice his horror:

There is another dress which is very ugly, for it makes women appear very fat and as wide as tongues. It is true that by nature women should be short, with slender or narrow shoulders, breasts and back, and small heads, and that their faces should be thin and small … and also that they should be wide and big round the back and belly and the hips so that they can have space for children they conceive and carry for nine months … But although this is true, the aforesaid dress greatly exceeds and more than greatly exceeds, the natural proportions, and instead of making woman beautiful and well-proportioned, makes them ugly, monstrous and deformed until they cease to look like women and look like bells …

'Verdugadas', 'vertugale' and the 'verdingale' derive from the Spanish word 'verdugos', meaning 'smooth twigs put out by a tree that has been cut or pruned', and relates to the fact that this new skirt was held away from the body by horizontal seams threaded through with wood. *(Author's collection)*

Finally, such dress is very deceitful and very ugly. It is in truth great deceit in a woman who is slender, hipless, and very thin, to give herself hips and a shape with cloth and wool; if carried out in moderation it might be overlooked and at most would be a venial sin. But done in such a way, without moderation and with exaggeration, it is undoubtedly a deception and a lie of great guilt and consequently a great sin … Thus it is a sin when women who are small of stature wear chopines to feign a height they do not possess, especially as Our Lord has willed it that women are usually short of body and smaller than men, since they have to be ruled by them as their superiors, or when they with rags, wool, petticoats or hoops, affect a width which they do not possess. There is no doubt that deception and lies are a moral sin when carried out in the above evil and sinful manner; thus the padded hips and hoop skirts are very harmful and very wicked garments; with reason they have been forbidden under pain of excommunication.

This dress did not just raise eyebrows in Spain. When it was introduced into Italy in 1498 it was immediately banned and in many towns abandoned altogether. It was England that embraced it in 1501 and until its eventual demise in the first decade of the seventeenth century it was worn by both commoner and queen alike.

Once the farthingale became the underskirt the material used in its construction became less important. No longer richly decorated, the choices of fabric were basically buckram and tuke, which were similar to canvas and therefore heavy enough to make the cone shape. Depending on finances, lightweight wool, taffeta or velvet could also be used and it's known that Queen Elizabeth I wore silk farthingales often edged with kersey – a type of wool – as a bottom border as it prolonged the life of the delicate fabric which was always in contact with the floor. The ropes – also known as bent ropes or bents – that held the farthingale out in its unique shape were also made from long lengths of the material, with a tailor named Walter Fyshe in 1560 using 7½yd of 'twisted' kersey, so as to give it the strength to make such ropes. It is also possible that the ropes were actually made of rope, though this may have proved to be too heavy. In 1565 the stiffening changed from twisted material to reeds, which were much lighter. In 1580 whalebone was also known to have been used.

Just as few would fail to recognise the early Tudor cone-shaped skirt for women and the wide, square profile for men, they would also fail to miss the other accessory that contributed to the distinctive silhouette – the sleeve. When Henry VIII penned his love for Anne Boleyn in the song 'Greensleeves' (thought to be his own work) he immortalised the humble sleeve, revering it as the embodiment of something far more precious. Yet, in Tudor times sleeves were precious. Detachable and therefore easily lost, sleeves and undersleeves – which resembled gauntlets – were taken care of and could make or break any outfit. Not just an integral part of a woman's garment, sleeves could be added to doublets and jerkins, usually pinned or tied, the fixings well concealed under padded 'wings' on the shoulder.

Sleeves were given as gifts, embroidered, quilted or slashed and were a thing apart, a totally independent item. Without rules that said a sleeve had to match their rich gown or peasant bodice, sleeves could be of any colour and often were. Fur was a popular adornment on sleeves, though it had to be worn in accordance with the sumptuary laws. These laws attempted to restrict the opulence of dress in order to curb extravagance and to stop moral decline. To the medieval and Tudor mind it was paramount they be able to distinguish at a single glance a milkmaid from a countess or a member of the merchant classes, who now rising swiftly within the class system had more money than blue blood. Surely if this was not possible the very fabric of society would unravel? Sumptuary laws were also there to protect fortunes, to stop the 'ruin of a multitude of serviceable young men and gentlemen of good families' by preventing them from squandering money on fashionable clothing and, as in a Statute of Apparel issued from Westminster dated

7 May 1562, to stop the 'decay of horses within the realm', as quoted in John Strype, *Annals of the Reformation and Establishment of Religion*, Vol. 2, Part 1. A strange connection one would think, but the Queen was insistent that every man should be capable of providing the country with the service of good horses should war arise. She was not about to tolerate those of her male subjects in an appropriate position to be unable to defend her realm by 'reason of his wife's apparel' or the fact she was allowed to spend too much on clothes she shouldn't be wearing anyway.

Of course dress could be elaborate if you were of the correct station in life and sleeves were a case in point to prove it. The fur that adorned the sleeves of the gentry or aristocratic ladies' 'trumpet' sleeves could be as exotic as Lucerne or lynx fur, genet, the fur of the civet cat, or Foins, the name given to the pelts of the more common weasel-like animal namely the beech marten. Slashed sleeves were popular in both Germany, France and England by the end of the 1520s and continued to be a favourite during the Elizabethan period until the end of the century.

From large items of clothing to small, sumptuary laws even dictated what feathers could and could not adorn one's hat, something everyone over the age of 13 was required to wear in public. Lower classes were allowed to wear plain feathers, such as goose, duck, chicken or grouse, while the middle classes and above could use expensive feathers, such as peacock, ostrich, egret and swan. As pheasants were considered a delicacy and were protected as game for the local nobility their feathers were restricted to the upper classes. Any commoner caught wearing a pheasant feather was labelled a 'poacher' and could be put to death. On festival days it was common for young unmarried girls to wear flower garlands in their hair.

Just like the codpiece, the doublet, a mainstay of male clothing in the sixteenth and seventeenth centuries, was also given to exaggeration. Beginning as a simple stitched and quilted double-layered lining which came to be known as 'doubling', it was worn to protect the skin under the chain mail or metal breastplate of medieval armour. From the late fifteenth century onward it emerged as a garment in its own right, and for the wealthy was something to be shaped and decorated to the extremes of Tudor fashion.

Basically unchanged for over 300 years, the doublet is easily recognised as a snug-fitting item which supported a man's hose, kept him warm and gave him shape, with the only difference down the years being its style and cut. Buttons down the front were the only fastenings, sleeves were generally attached (unlike women's), they had collars and depending on the era decorative tabs at the waist and/or shoulder. Materials available to make a doublet were varied but then, as now, were possibly budget driven with varieties of leathers, velvets and silks for the rich and linen, hemp, canvas, fustian, cotton and wool blends or broadcloths for the rest. For working people the doublet would rarely be stiffened, or over padded, as it would hinder free movement but for those whose clothing was 'state of the art' they were highly decorated, with fine needlework and embroidery and adorned with jewels, spangles and pearls.

The 'slashed' or 'pinked' doublet became a favourite. Rich linings worn beneath were pulled through the slash or diamond-shaped cuts then puffed out to emphasise colour and fabric. Ideas abound as to just what triggered this flamboyant ornamentation, the most popular being that Swiss and Bavarian mercenaries, more popularly known as Landsknecht or Lansquenet, in 1477 mended their tattered uniforms with strips of fabric from the banners and pennants from the tents of a vanquished enemy. Another suggestion is that after a battle the soldiers could only be paid with the spoils of a city, which happened to be sumptuous cloth with which they plugged the holes of their tattered clothing thus creating the multi-coloured attire. Whatever the reason for the custom, by 1520 the fashion had spread across Europe, with tunics, gowns, hats, bodices and doublets for both men and women receiving this treatment, the luxurious fabrics on display via the decorative slashes known as 'pullings' or 'drawings out'.

Doublets were styled to demonstrate masculinity with emphasis on broad shoulders and slim hips, sometimes with 'girdles', the equivalent of the later female corset, worn to achieve the

Lanzichenecchi at the Battle of Pavia, 1525. *(Author's collection)*

The German Landsknecht or Lansquenet were colourful mercenary soldiers with a formidable reputation. Their elaborate dress, which was deliberately slashed at the front, back and sleeves, singled them out and was, it is thought, the inspiration for the slashed doublets and hose of the Tudor and Elizabethan periods. *(Author's collection)*

ultimate triangular silhouette. A deviation from this, and no doubt a godsend to the male corset wearers, was the peascod, or goose-bellied doublet, which came to England from Holland in the 1570s and was stuffed in such a way as to give a man the impression of having a small, pointed paunch. Just as such dress seems strange to modern eyes it appeared no less ridiculous to Philip Stubbes, a stout Puritan in thought, deed and dress, whose book *The Anatomie of Abuses* was to social comment in the sixteenth century what newspapers and magazines are today. Unimpressed with the pigeon-chested fashion, he criticised the offending doublet as being so 'harde-quilted, and stuffed, bombasted and sewed, as they can neither woorke, nor yet well plaie in them'. He also pointed out that these garments could be nothing if not excessively hot and it was almost impossible to 'eyther stoupe downe, or bowe themselves to the grounde, soe styffe and sturdy they stand about them'. Needless to say, he failed to see any 'handsomnes to be found in such dublettes', supposing those who depicted themselves with such great bellies to be men inclined only gluttony.

To 'turn a fine leg' was also the intention of every sixteenth- and seventeenth-century gentleman, the opportunity to do just that presenting itself once knee-length Tudor hose began to rise sharply from the bottom up stopping eventually at thigh level. Whereas at the start of the century all emphasis was on the chest, by its close this had changed radically. Men wore sleek upper body garments with puffed lower body garments designed to emphasise the leg in hose. Unlike the Middle Ages when hose were purely a leg covering, now they had separated into two garments: upper hose or breeches and nether hose or stockings.

Stubbes also had plenty to say in his usual long-winded way about what he considered excesses in clothing, this time turning his attention to men's hose and their numerous names. To be fair, there were many hose from which to choose. Trunk hose were very short and padded over a full inner layer or lining. 'Slops' were loose, very full breeches that reached just below the knee, with highly decorative bands of material called guardes. Galligaskin or gally-hose breeches from Gascony again reaching below the knee. There were French hose, semi-fitted breeches coming to below the knee and decorated with costly ornaments, worn by nobility and the upper classes, and common French hose, largely unadorned, round, long, broad and wide and worn by the lower classes. Lastly but not least there were plunderhosen, a form of 'slops' with a very full inner layer pulled out between the panes and hanging below the knee which originated in Germany.

Stubbes also pointed out that things had definitely got out of hand where men's clothing was concerned. He cited that in past times even kings were happy to wear a pair of hose that cost no more than 'tenne Shillinges, or a Marke', but now even gentry thought nothing of 'bestowin twentie nobles, ten pound, twentie pound, fortie pound, yea, a hundred pound on one paire of Breeches!'. Such were the liberties taken with men's hose and other apparel that it was feared the lack of respect for one's station would bring about civil unrest. On 6 May 1562, by advice of her Council and 'upon the Queen's Majesty's commandment', Elizabeth I revised several of her sumptuary laws.

It was decreed that as the 'monstrous and outrageous greatness of hose' had crept 'of late into the realm' it was, from the day of the order, illegal for any tailor or hosier to use any more than 1¾yd of material to make any one pair of hose and that the lining should only be of one kind. Such linings were not to be loose or bolstered, 'but to lie just unto their legs', in other words a man was not to be so vain as to use his hose to ostentatiously display his wealth or to attract the ladies. This was obviously ignored by one young man who having shied away from using the usual wadding or 'bombast' (from which derives the word bombastic – meaning overblown) had stuffed the lining of his short trunk hose with bran to increase their size. Exchanging pleasantries with several ladies who by their smiles and giggles he presumed were enjoying his company, he continued his engaging conversation no doubt planning the seduction of one of the ladies at a later hour. Unfortunately, all was not as it seemed as unbeknown to him he had at an earlier point snagged

Sir Walter Raleigh and his son display a 'fine leg' in trunk hose. *(Courtesy of the National Portrait Gallery)*

his trunk hose on a wayward nail and the ladies were coquettishly laughing, alas not at his witty banter but at a small heap of bran steadily growing in size on the floor beside him. Eventually realising his predicament, he made a hurried escape with both his ego and his hose deflating at an alarming rate. To ensure hose were properly 'policed' the Mayor of London ordered that civil officers of Westminster and outlaying towns and villages were appointed to interview all hosiers or tailors and explain the new rules applying to the size of gentlemen's hose. It was suggested in no uncertain terms that should an individual not comply with the new ruling he would be heavily fined and 'suffered no more to continue his occupation'. These new officers would also be responsible for the apprehension, examination and committing to prison of the offenders.

The codpiece already mentioned in the previous chapter changed dramatically in the Tudor period. From a mere means of preserving a man's modesty it became a prominent feature of a man's wardrobe. The fashion spanned all age groups and lasted from the 1540s to the 1590s, and though a common accompaniment to male costume of the time, to the modern mind it is an object both strange yet compelling. So what made the Tudor codpiece so different from its predecessor? Was it a sex promotion object, a statement of virility and competition or just a natural progression of a fashion item?

In Italy, the codpiece was called a *sacco* and in France a *braguette*. As time passed the object became shaped and padded, designed to emphasise rather than to conceal, reaching its peak in terms of size and decoration in the 1540s. Highly decorative they were often be-decked with ribbons and bows, while some were even used to hold money and other small valuable items. Its eventual rigid structure was achieved by stuffing a soft fabric with straw or horsehair or it was moulded into harder shapes by using buckram or leather. Speculation has it that the roomy space inside offered protection from all the things hanging from a man's belt, including swords, daggers and hard purses.

It was also thought that men whose virility was in question sported the biggest and most decorative codpieces to emphasise their masculinity. Holbein, for example, painted Henry VIII as a broad-shouldered, lusty male, his majestic presence conveyed through his aggressive posture and the fact he was wearing a codpiece. The portrait was actually painted during his brief marriage to Jane Seymour, *c.* 1536/7, and when he had just fathered his only living son at the age of 45. Was the portrait and Henry's codpiece a psychological reaffirmation of his virility? Was he, even as king, a man who needed to substantiate the fact that he could father children and dare others to question his fertility? Large decorative codpieces, of course, also hid the devastating effects of syphilis. Scholars agree it is unlikely Henry VIII died of the disease as none of his living children – Mary Tudor, Henry Fitzroy, Duke of Richmond, Elizabeth I and Edward VI – exhibited any form of congenital syphilis. Also, no records have been found showing that his doctors prescribed medication for it. But others who suffered the effects of the scourge of the times possibly utilised the codpiece as a perfect disguise.

Known as the Great Pox, syphilis had always had its place in the ancient world but reached epidemic proportions in the sixteenth century in Europe. It was something nobody wished to lay claim to. Italians called it the *Mal Françoise*, the English referred to it as the French Pox and the French the *Mal de Naples*. Not wishing the finger of blame to be pointed at them, the Flemish ultimately blamed Spain. Whoever's fault it was the disease as described in 1546 by poet/physician Fracastor made those affected 'sad, weary, and cast-down'. This is not surprising given that sores, small at first, but persistent, covered the genital organs 'constantly discharging an incredible quantity of stinking matter'. The treatment was a mixture of medical observation, animal grease and mercury that was applied as a paste to the affected area, which was afterwards wrapped in bulky bandages resulting in difficulty walking and urinating as well as a tell-tale frontal bulge. The codpiece would have been able to work on two levels, both as a container for greasy ointments which would stain outer clothing and disguise the bandages and it allowed the

Family of Henry VIII, *c*. 1545. *(Courtesy of T.P. Campbell,* Henry VIII and the Art of Majesty, *New Haven and London, 2007)*

afflicted to be camouflaged among his friends at a time when wearing codpieces was universal. Most men were eventually worn out by the toxic effects of mercury and died. For centuries after the old adage of 'One night with Venus, six months with Mercury' was a warning to those about to embark upon numerous sexual encounters.

The codpiece was incorporated into armour as much as a sign of masculinity as for protection. *(Author's collection)*

Codpieces also found their way into armour of the sixteenth century and so for a time were an addition to the best full harnesses. Whether they were actually worn was another matter as sitting astride a horse wearing one would have been nothing if not uncomfortable. To all intents and purposes the area in question could have just as well been protected by chain mail which was flexible.

Writing in 1532, François Rabelais, a writer, doctor, humanist, monk and scholar, venerates the codpiece in his book the *Histories of Gargantua and Pantagruel*, a humorous and bawdy tale, by greatly inflating its importance. He exalts the codpiece as 'the chief piece of a military harness', equating it with how nature has equipped all manner of things with their own protective 'codpieces' by 'strengthening, covering, guarding, and fortifying them with husks, cases, scurfs and swads, hulls, cods, stones, films, cartels, shells, ears, rinds, barks, skins, ridges, and prickles, which serve them instead of strong, fair, and natural codpieces …'. He then goes on to explain that nature has been unfair to man creating him 'naked, tender, and frail, without either offensive or defensive arms'. An obvious disadvantage, this necessitates him to then 'put on arms, and make provision of harness against wars and violence'. He concludes, 'if the ballocks be marred, the whole race of human kind would forthwith perish, and be lost for ever'.

As if to underline this sentiment, Rabelais continues with the example of the importance of manly protection by citing Lord Humphrey de Merville, who when summoned to follow his King to war tried on a new suit of armour. At the same time his wife was contemplating the fact that he was covering all of his body against attack, except for what she considered a most precious ingredient to their marriage. She then scolded him for having 'but small care of the staff of love and packet of marriage' by not covering them with 'links of mail', and offered to give him an old tilting helmet she had lying in her closet with which to 'shield, fence, and gabionate' his genitalia. Rabelais then adds a verse which ultimately marks her concern:

> When Yoland saw her spouse equipp'd for fight,
> And, save the codpiece, all in armour dight,
> My dear, she cried, why, pray, of all the rest
> Is that exposed, you know I love the best?
> Was she to blame for an ill-managed fear,—
> Or rather pious, conscionable care?
> Wise lady, she! In hurly-burly fight,
> Can any tell where random blows may light?

The codpiece became part of the male costume out of necessity but also became a visual suggestion of masculinity and virility for over half a century. Some protruded at preposterous angles and were stuffed upright, some were padded and used as secret hiding places for items of value, giving rise to the age-old double entendre of keeping safe the 'family jewels'. With some of the most powerful men of the age, Francis I, Emperor Charles V and Henry VIII, appearing in portraits which included codpieces it can be can be assumed the fashion had become an intrinsic part of the late-medieval male psyche and symbolic of male conquest, prowess and dominance over his new and expanding world. By the time Queens Mary and Elizabeth of England came to the throne the fashion had disappeared into the ever more voluminous folds of colourful trunk hose.

Elizabethan and late Tudor colours were a varied affair and as dyes became more accessible there was always a pressure to invent accurate names. Some colours were self-explanatory, such as 'ash' used for commoners' gowns and kirtles along with a grey called 'rats'. 'Puke' was a dirty brown colour and 'goose-turd green' not difficult to imagine. Russet was the same then as it is now, but plum was called 'murrey' and golden-brown was 'tawney'. Other yellow shades were named after what they resembled such as 'primrose' or 'straw', with tan shades named as 'maiden hair' for a bright shade and 'Isabella' for a light buff. A very light yellow was known as 'cane'.

Red was associated with power and importance and this colour clothing was described as being for all valiant men, including such shades as 'Bristol red', a light red called 'lustie-gallant', a blood red called 'sangyn' and 'strammel', a name first coined in 1575. In 1552 King Edward VI decreed that only the following colours were to be made that year: 'scarlet', 'crimson', 'murrey', 'sheep's colour' (a natural shade), 'puke', 'orange-tawney', 'watchet' (blue) and 'lion's colour' (a yellowish tan), 'marble', 'sad new colour', 'motley' and 'iron grey'. What these colours looked like has as yet not been fully researched. Edward also had favourite colours, which were 'incarnate' (red), 'carnation' (resembled the colour of raw flesh), 'blod' (possibly a blood red), 'turkey' and 'sea-water'. In 1554 Mary Tudor's preferred shades were 'ruby', 'crane' (greyish white) and 'old medley', of which little is presently known.

Blue became an interesting phenomenon at this time with indigo widely available, inexpensive and easy to transport in the form of dye-cakes. Also, it was relatively permanent compared to many other dyestuffs of the time. As a result, it became a popular dye for the clothing of servants and others of a lower station and began the tradition for blue to be associated with the state of servitude. 'Plunket', 'watchet', 'whey' and 'milk and water' were light blue, a blue/green, a pale greenish-blue and whitish-blue respectively. Long fine blue also existed.

Despite the fanciful names littering the dye books of this era, scholars today have still to research them fully. 'Dead Spaniard', 'The Devil in the Head', 'Ape's Laugh', 'Mortal Sin' and 'pease-Porrige Tawnie' conjure up a myriad of suggestions with 'Love Longing', 'Kiss Me Darling' and 'dawn' promising to be colours of a more pleasing hue. As for others of this period, namely, 'scratch face', 'smoked Ox', 'merry widow', 'resurrection', 'brown bread' and 'dying Monkey', one can only imagine!

CHAPTER 4

Drums and Wheels

'The women, when they have all these goodly robes upon them, seem to be the smallest part of themselves, not natural women, but artificial women; not women of flesh and blood, but rather puppets or mawmuts, consisting of rags and clouts compact together.'

Stubbes, *The Anatomie of Abuses*

Keeping one's head upon one's neck had been a major concern for those connected to the Tudor court, and as the days of Henry VIII waned and the golden age of his daughter Elizabeth dawned the throat became once more the focus of attention. It was not so much a question of the neck being exposed upon a block, but it being completely concealed. Along with the Spanish farthingale, the wasp-waist corset and trunk hose, the ruff is possibly the first item that springs to mind when people consider Elizabethan costume. Large ruffs were the despair of laundresses as often these were held away from the wearer's face by hundreds of carefully inserted sticks of wood or bone, and could only be worn once before they had to be washed, ironed and refolded, the tiny sticks painstakingly reinserted. This was to change in 1564 with the arrival of Mistress Dinghen Van Der Plasse, who essentially taught the English how to make starch – a word derived from Middle English 'sterchen' meaning to stiffen.

Despite its preposterous dimensions during its heyday, the 'ruff' had humble beginnings when in the 1530s and 40s it was no more than a simple frill on the collar and cuffs of a chemise. As the fashion became popular and independent of other garments ruffs could be washed, starched and set into elaborate figure-of-eight folds by using cone-shaped goffering irons, and setting-sticks. 'Poking-sticks' were heated in the fire and applied to the folds of the ruff, in effect ironing it into the precise symmetry so admired in the 1500s. Starch began to be used, but only on a small scale and with some recipes being more successful than others. It was only after the young refugee Mistress Dinghen Van Der Plasse had fled her native Flanders for her 'better safetie' and settled in London's Cheapside that starch-making underwent a revolution. Tutored since the age of 12 in the art of ruff-making by her late father, she used her extensive needlework skills to create ruffs stiffened with starch taken from a secret recipe which used as its main agent the bluebell plant. Soon her new 'clear' starch was in great demand as it did not clog-up the loose weave of delicate muslins and other fabrics with unsightly granules, giving her ruffs a much-desired crisp finish.

Mistress Van Der Plasse became a very successful business woman. Patronised by Queen Elizabeth's household which employed her methods, it wasn't long before starching houses sprang up all over England despite religious conservatives branding her worse than a witch and her clear-starch mixture the 'Devil's broth'. Women in general who had made their own ruffs took the liberty of sending them to her workshop in order for them to be starched, as observed by one London resident:

Ruffs became 'monstrous' in size and were legislated against in Tudor England. From *Illustrated London News*, 1858. *(Author's collection)*

The most curious wives now made for themselves ruffs of cambric, & sent them to Mrs Dinghen to be starched, who charged high prices; after a time made themselves ruffs of lawn; & thereupon arose a general scoff or by-word that shortly they would make their ruffs of spiders' web. Mrs Dinghen at last took their daughters as her pupils; her usual terms were four or five pounds for teaching them to starch, & one pound for the art of seething starch.

Of course, where there are means extravagance often follows, born out by the enormous lengths (and breadths) the ruff went on to assume. One particular gauzy creation was all of 'a quarter of a yard' but appeared to be something designers were reluctant to claim. In England it was commonly known as the 'French Ruff', whereas in France it was referred to as 'the English Monster'! At their most extreme, ruffs were a foot or more wide and needed a wire frame called a supportasse or underpropper to hold them at a fashionable angle. Of course, there were those who deplored the fashion and, as one would expect, the Puritan Philip Stubbes made his views known in 1583 in *The Anatomie of Abuses*:

The women use great ruffes, & neckerchers of holland, lawne, camerick, & such cloth, as the greatest thred shall not be so bigge as the leasthaire that is: then, least they should fall

32

down, they are smeared & starched in the devils liquore, I meane Starch: after that, dryed with great diligence, streaked, patted & rubbed very nicely, & so applyed to their goodly necks, &, withall, underpropped with supportasses (as I tolde you before) the stately arches of pride: beyond all this they have a further fetch, nothing inferiour to the rest; as, namely, three or foure degrees of minor ruffes, placed gradatim, step by step, one beneath the other, & all under the Maister devil ruffe. The skyrts, then, of these great ruffes are long & wide every way, pleted & crested ful curiously, Godwot.

Ecclesiastics were not enamoured with them either with the Bishop of London, John King, condemning them from the pulpit with, 'Fashion brought in deep ruffs & shallow ruffs, thick ruffs & thin ruffs, double ruffs & no ruffs. When God shall come to judge the quick & the dead, he will not know those who have so defaced the fashion he hath erected'. The Revd Hall, Bishop of Exeter, finishing a sermon on the vanities of 'farthingales, feathers, and paint' concluded with, 'Hear this, ye popinjays of our time; hear this, ye plaster faced Jezabels: God will one day wash them with fire & with brimstone.'

Towards the end of the 1500s, fashion dictated a more feminine fan-shaped ruff, which was achieved by opening the ruffle in front to expose the neck and cleavage. This was often constructed on gauze wings raised at the back of the head which allowed greater movement of the neck. As sour as always, Philip Stubbes' Puritan outlook caused him to comment on this openly seductive accessory: 'Sometimes they are pinned up to their eares, sometimes they are suffered to hang over their shoulders, like windmil sayles fluttering in the winde; & thus every one pleaseth herself with her foolish devices, for as the proverb saith: "everyone thinketh his own wayes best"'.

Condemnation is rarely a reason for the fashion conscious to conform to the norm and so Queen Elizabeth eventually legislated against various items of dress, for example, ruffs and rapiers that served to over-inflate the egos of many of her subjects. At one point there were even studious and sober citizens placed at each one of London's city gates to cut the ruffs and to break off rapier points of all that exceeded a yard's length or a 'nail of a yard' in the depth of their ruffs. It appears that in France laws were not as stringent, as it was rumoured that in 1579 Queen Margot, 1st wife of Henry IV of France (1533–1615), when seated at dinner, was obliged to have a spoon with a handle 2ft long for the purpose of passing her soup over her ruff, so as to keep it rigid and immaculate.

The ruff, as well as being perhaps *the* most recognisable item of the Elizabethan age, dictated the hairstyles of both men and women, most famously short hair for men with a pointed beard, and provided a perfect frame for the face; a face enhanced by what can only be described as deadly make-up. With the Tudors believing that 'outward beauty was a true sign of inner godliness', Elizabeth I's first appearance on the world stage saw her appear as a virgin queen with her hair flowing and an alabaster complexion, the latter being the result of white lead make-up also known as ceruse. The cult of Gloriana had arrived.

Elizabeth knew that beauty was powerful and inspired devotion in return, which, due to a turbulent and insecure childhood, she craved. It was not enough for her to *be* queen she wanted to be *seen to be* queen which in an age devoid of media meant she often rode among her people, her face perfectly painted. This was an invitation to her subjects to love her and therefore be less inclined to rebel against her. It was Elizabeth's aim to make herself more than a weak and feeble woman and using cosmetics was part of the ruse. Just as her father had famously put himself above the Church, in this matter so did Elizabeth. The Church decried the use of make-up and Philip Stubbes in *The Anatomie of Abuses* echoed the stance the Church took on such things: 'a woman through painting and dying her face, sheweth herself to be more then [sic] whorish. For she hath corrupted and defaced (like a filthie strumpet or brothel) the workmanship of God in her ...'.

Queen Elizabeth portrayed as
'Wisdom' in an antique print, 1898.
(Author's collection)

Elizabeth was determined to cover the scars she had received from her bout of smallpox in 1562 and so defied those that condemned cosmetics and became a devotee of the smoothing coverage of white lead. There were other powders available, such as ground alabaster or starch, but they did not produce the perfect luminosity she favoured nor gave the coverage she needed. Rouge, usually of red ochre, would be applied to re-introduce the faded bloom of youth, and lips would be coloured with a 'crayon' of ground alabaster or plaster of Paris mixed with either cochineal or dyes from the East Indian brazil tree, all mixed together and dried into sticks in the sun. An egg-white glaze was finally applied, covering everything with a porcelain-like shine. Cosmetics were usually home-made but there were ready-made products to be had, some infused, so it was rumoured, with magical powers. There was even a sixteenth-century 'chemical peel' advocated by physician and alchemist Ruscelli. He recommended that a woman use eggs, vinegar, turpentine, camphor, rock alum, quicksilver, lemon juice, tartarum and white onion mixed into a paste and applied to the neck, breast and face letting it 'drie of itself, at night when you goe to bedde …'. There was, however, a drawback as the concoction had to be left in place for no less than 'eight daise …' then removed via another complicated recipe before steaming the face.

Elizabeth firmly believed that beauty and strength were one and the same and so thought England's success as a nation was a reflection of her ability to be beautiful. To stay so she employed

Catherine of Aragon (1485–1536) in the 'Gable Hood' of the late Medieval and early Tudor period. Artist unknown. *(Author's collection)*

more and more ceruse which ironically ate into the flesh it was supposed to be smoothing, forcing her to poison that on which, in her eyes, England depended.

Just as the verdingale had dictated the female shape from its introduction in England by Catherine of Aragon seventy years previously, by 1577 a new version of the farthingale had been sent to the Queen and came to embody the Elizabethan era. Called the half-farthingale, it was a design that allowed the front of the dress to fall flat while only the sides and back of the dress were filled out. Known to be a thrifty housekeeper, Queen Elizabeth resisted having too many new outfits made, preferring instead to have many of her old farthingales altered and on many occasions repaired. Her Wardrobe Accounts feature many entries for payments made to various dressmakers and seamstresses, not least her favourite tailor Robert Sibthorpe, who in 1586 was paid for 'alteringe enlarginge & styffenynge of seven half verthingalls iii of satten' and again in 1591 paid for 'alteringe and newe coueringe of iiii half verthingales of Taffata with whales bones'. Though generally constant in shape, farthingales were often widened requiring more panels to be added, or decreased with panels being removed.

The last style of the farthingale before its demise in the early decades of the seventeenth century was the 'cart-wheel', 'Catherine-wheel' or 'drum' farthingale. As England stood proud in her achievements as a nation so too this strange skirt stood proud of the body, surrounding it in a stiff, unyielding circle before allowing the costume to fall vertically to the ankles. It is described by Jane Ashelford in her book *The Art of Dress*:

The structure carried the skirt out to right angles from the waist to a width varying from 8 to 48-inches before falling vertically to the ground. To avoid the hard line made by the rim of the wheel farthingale, the skirt was given a circular frill or flounce, the pleats of which radiated out from the centre to the edge of the rim. The whole skirt was then tilted at the waist so that the hem was raised at the back and lowered in the front. Wearing the farthingale at this angle allowed the wearer to rest her hands on the ledge-like surface of the flounce …

The way in which this farthingale was worn created the illusion of a long torso and shorter legs, which alluded to, in the case of younger women, a childbearing figure. To add to the illusion and help support the creation and keep it stable it was worn over a bum-roll. Lower class women wore a much larger bum-roll to imitate the fashion of the higher classes as they could not afford a full farthingale. Lastly, it was worn under what we today have come to know as a corset but before the eighteenth century in England (the French were using the word as early as 1611) was called a 'pair of bodies', the name thought to originate from a time when the garment was actually two separate parts laced together front and back. In 1577 an account by Jerome Lippomano, a French ambassador, documented the inconceivably narrow waists of his native French women, commenting on how they swelled out their gowns from the waist downwards 'by whaleboned stuffs and vertugadins, which increases the elegance of their figures. Over the chemise they wear a corset of bodice, that they call a 'corps pique', which makes their shape more delicate and slender. It is fastened behind which helps to show off the form of the bust.' Proof that the purpose

A cone-shaped bodice typical of the Tudor period and seen here with a bum-roll. *(Photograph Tessa Hallmann)*

Back view. *(Photograph Tessa Hallmann)*

of the 'bodies' was to support and flatten the front of the torso.

It has become the norm to think of a 'pair of bodies' (corset) as an Elizabethan undergarment but this was not strictly the case, the only real underwear being the shift or chemise. Bodies were worn under other garments, but not as nineteenth-century corsets were worn, crisp, white and never meaning to be seen. The rich, able to wear multiple finely decorated layers, would have worn a doublet over the corset when receiving any but the most intimate visitors. The middle classes, on the other hand, wore the bodies as a top garment with the addition of sleeves and a cloak, if necessary, when they went out. Decorated and made from attractive coloured fabrics, they were intended to be seen.

Wearing a farthingale necessitated certain ways of holding oneself as the stiffness of Elizabethan clothing made a relaxed posture impossible. A lady could rest her wrists upon the edge, or upon the swell of the garment with arms held away from the body and her elbows bent outward to emphasise a narrow waist. Corsets pushed the breasts high and the shoulders back forcing the head into a poised position often mistaken as haughty. Though it may seem unacceptable to us today to accept such uncomfortable costumes, the sixteenth-century woman knew no different and so accepted what she wore as the norm.

Throughout the use of the farthingale, sitting was generally a difficult matter; chairs were simply not wide enough, so cushions were used. Skirts and farthingale were lifted over the pile of cushions and then the lady was free to sit down, encompassed by the skirts. At a party held by Queen Elizabeth in May of 1559 many of her ladies-in-waiting had to sit on the ground because of the lack of room at the table. An observer of the feast wrote:

> The supper hour having arrived … The Queen, having washed her hands, and being at table under her canopy, insisted on having M. de Mountmorency at her little table … At the large table all the rest of the French lords and gentlemen sat on one side, and on the other all the ladies, of whom there was no small number, and who required so much space on account of the farthingales they wore that there was not room for all; so part of the Privy Chamber ate on the ground on the rushes, being excellently served by lords and cavaliers, who gave them courage and company at their repast.

Costume did eventually dictate the design of furniture and the farthingale chair was created. This was an armless chair with a wide seat covered in high-quality fabric, fitted with a cushion and a backrest with an upholstered panel. Able to accommodate a woman's wide skirts, it was one of the earliest comfortable upholstered seats introduced as a lady's chair in the late sixteenth century, though not named until much later in the nineteenth century. An earlier English name was 'imbrauderer's chair' or 'upholsterer's chair'.

CHAPTER 5

Sumptuous Stuarts

'Be it resolved that all women, of whatever age, rank, profession, or degree; whether virgin maids or widows; that shall after the passing of this Act, impose upon and betray into matrimony any of His Majesty's male subjects, by scents, paints, cosmetics, washes, artificial teeth, false hair, Spanish wool, iron stays, hoops, high-heeled shoes, or bolstered hips, shall incur the penalty of the laws now in force against witchcraft, sorcery, and such like misdemeanours, and that the marriage, upon conviction, shall stand null and void.'

Bill from the British Parliament, 1690

With the death of Elizabeth I the age of Gloriana began to fade. The wondrous era of power and prestige was giving way to the more circumspect reign of a dour king with fashions changing little during the opening decade of the seventeenth century. Elizabeth's fashions, at least for women, persisted for a time beyond her death as ladies, who took their cues from royalty, were to see the old queen's nephew James I give over the whole of her late majesty's huge and costly wardrobe to his wife, Anne, upon his succession to the throne. This was for Anne, as with any woman, to prove a mixed blessing, for as reluctant as she was to receive cast-offs (albeit those of a queen), Anne knew her husband for a parsimonious individual and was often kept short of her clothes allowance. Elizabeth's wardrobe inventory, however, proved the garments were no mean gift as it was said she had 102 French gowns (gowns with a slight train in the back), 100 loose gowns (gowns worn in private chambers without a corset), 67 round gowns (gowns without trains), 99 robes, 127 cloaks, 85 doublets, 125 petticoats, 56 safeguards (outer skirts), 126 kirtles and 136 stomachers.

Female dress still enthusiastically embraced the farthingale, which although a mode of dress accepted by all in the Western world apparently still produced surprise in far-flung corners of the globe. An entry in a book by John Bulwer, an English physician and philosopher, called *A Pedigree of a Gallant* recounts how James I upon sending his envoy, Sir Peter Wyatt, as ambassador to Constantinople also allowed his wife to accompany him, her gentlewomen, in turn accompanying her. On their arrival the wife of the Sultan wished to meet the ladies from across the sea and arranged an audience. Lady Wyatt clearly surprised the Sultaness with her huge and decorated appearance and was asked to explain her costume, as it was clear the Sultaness had never seen women dressed like that before. It was a strange phenomenon and the author went on to explain that whereas Eastern women have always followed 'a simple ideal of dress' and had never 'wandered into the follies and distortions of the European ladies', it was, however, the ladies of the European world who despised their Eastern neighbours.

The period was also a turning point for the wearing of ruffs and bands. These quickly fell out of favour as the reign continued, especially those, and there were many, that were stiffened with yellow starch. This can be attributed to a particular incident, the murder of Sir Thomas Overbury.

Anne of Denmark (1574–1619), wife of James I, who inherited a large part of Queen Elizabeth I's wardrobe. The painting, attributed to John de Critz, *c.* 1605, shows her wearing a wheel or drum farthingale. *(Courtesy of the National Portrait Gallery)*

It was not he that wore the ruff in question but a Mrs Anne Turner, a milliner's wife of Paternoster Row, who as an accomplice to the Countess of Somerset (herself pardoned due to high-ranking connections) was complicit in the crime. When Anne was hanged at Tyburn she was wearing a yellow cobweb-lawn ruff.

Fashion at this time was no less 'complicated' than it had been before except now there were no longer any sumptuary laws. In 1604, a year into King James's reign, Parliament had decided against all further statutes of apparel, thinking all men perfectly able to dress themselves accordingly, preferring to issues royal decrees if there was a need to curb extravagance or for political reasons, but these were few and far between. It was thought in this new and forward-thinking seventeenth century that sumptuary legislation was rooted in the Middle Ages and that there was no longer a great need for such medieval fondness for regulation. Perhaps the legislators had learned that such laws were very difficult to enforce, that it interfered too much with daily life, was oppressive and therefore liable to stir up discontent. Certainly, the demise of the sumptuary law could not be attributed to any decrease in extravagance, or by the disappearance of fantastic fashions. On the contrary, as far as britches were concerned they continued to be stuffed and displayed as they had in Elizabeth's time, giving rise to a satirical ballad entitled 'a Lamentable Complaint of the poore Cuntrye men, agaynste great hose, for the loss of their cattelles tales'; horsehair, and anything else that was handy, seems to have been used to stuff these capacious garments.

Perhaps as a result of the new dress freedom, overdressing became quite common.

In a sermon preached at Whitehall on the occasion of the marriage of Lord Hay (6 January 1607) the preacher, Robert Wilkinson, used the occasion to voice his own thoughts on women's fashion to a captive audience:

> Of all qualities, a woman must not have one qualitie of a ship, and that is too much rigging. Oh, what a wonder it is to see a ship under saile, with her tacklings and her masts, and her tops and top-gallants; Yea, but what a world of wonders it is to see a woman … so … deformed with her French, her Spanish, and her foolish fashions, that he that made her, when he looks upon her, shall hardly know her, with her plumes, her fannes, and a silken vizard, with a ruffe like a saile, yea a ruffe like a rainebow, with a feather in her cap like a flag in her top, to tell, I thinke, which way the wind will blow.

As if to add weight to Wilkinson's tirade, one playwright, who employed twelve maids to dress the young boy who was to play a female lead in his production, similarly observed and could not believe the rigmarole and time it took to make the lad ready:

> Such a stir, with combs, cascanets, dressing purls, fall squares, busks, bodies, scarfs, necklaces, carconets, sabatoes, borders, tires, fans, palisades, puffs, ruffs, cuffs, muffs, pushes, partlets, ringlets, bandlets, corslets, pendulets, armlets, bracelets … and also fardingales, kirtles, busks, points, shoe ties, and the like, that seven pedlars, shops, nay all Satrbridge Fair, will scarcely furnish her. A ship is sooner rigged by far than a gentlewoman made ready!

Barnabe Rich, another contemporary writer, commented in his *Honestie of this Age* in 1614 that seeing women going to church 'so paynted: periwigd: poudered: perfumed: starched: laced, and imbrodered' it was difficult 'to distinguish between a good woman and a bad'.

Fashion, during the Stuart era would evolve quite distinctly no less than four times with early styles still stiff, tight and heavily embellished. By 1620 clothing was becoming softer, less structured and comparatively more comfortable. Padding on both doublets and bodices disappeared and upstanding ruffs were replaced with falling bands sometimes known as Bertha collars. Waistlines both on men's and women's garments rose as did women's sleeves, allowing more flesh to be seen first at the wrist then the entire forearm.

With the death of James I English fashions mirrored those of France, most likely due to the fact that the new King, James' son, Charles I, had married the French Princess Henrietta Maria. Before long the stiff formality of the Spanish, which had influenced our clothing since the arrival of Catherine of Aragon and her vardingale, gave way to the subtlety and freer styles of Paris and Versailles. Unfortunately, not all saw this as liberating or welcome with an anonymous contemporary writer declaring that to his mind his fellow countrymen had turned 'French apes', and wore nothing but French styles: 'Wee are so disfigured by phantasticall end strange fashions that wee can scarce know him to daie, with whom wee were acquainted yesterdaie.' He also pointed out that 'some in the midst of winter wore doublets so cut and slashed that they could not keep in the body heat or keep out the rain!'. It was also commented upon that women frequently cut their dresses so low that their breasts and shoulders were practically entirely uncovered. This was considered 'an exorbitant and shameful enormity' which was prejudicial to the health, 'as by exposing too much to the cold, so that some of them lost the use of their hands and arms'. Not all females, it transpired, succumbed to this fashion, it apparently being only the plump and buxom who liberally displayed their bosoms. For those who were lean and far less well endowed it was equally noted that they went 'muffled up to the throat'.

With French cities now the leading producers of luxury goods, the fact they rigorously exported their silks and brocades did much to expand their influence. One such luxury item that was to epitomise the seventeeth century, whether made at home or across the Channel, was lace.

Lace – 'She herself has told me that lace is worn in hell', Don Quixote

The English word lace is derived from the Latin word *lacis*, meaning noose. Whereas Tudor lace was predominately 'net' lace, fashionable laces of the seventeenth and eighteenth centuries used bobbins or needles to create the intricate and fine web-like patterns. Aristocrats mortgaged estates for the want of it, just as the poor laboured, often by candlelight, to produce it. Smugglers risked their lives to obtain it, while women and children were transported to worlds beyond the seas for stealing a handkerchief's worth.

Adequate lighting was an important consideration in lace-making. In summer the cottagers could work outside, but at night and during the winter work was done by candlelight, which could be magnified by putting water into a glass vessel and shining a candle through it. Also in winter, to keep warm, 'fire-pots' were used. Women could not sit near fires because the smoke would dirty the expensive lace thread, so earthenware vessels pierced with holes and filled with hot ashes or glowing charcoal, were placed near their feet or tucked beneath their voluminous skirts.

Sometimes lace-makers would work in the lofts above cattle byres in winter. Heat generated by the bodies and breath of the animals stabled below would rise and help keep the workers warm. Even in such primitive conditions good workers would keep their hands scrupulously clean in order not to soil the lace and so lower its value.

Like a finely spun cobweb, lace became an integral part of the second fashion change to take place in the seventeenth century, namely the Cavalier period which began with the reign of King Charles I of England in 1625. In 1651 Jacob Van Eyck wrote:

Of many Arts, one surpasses all. For the maiden seated at her work flashes the smooth balls and thousand threads into the circle, and from this, her amusement, makes as much profit

Henrietta Maria, wife of Charles I, by Anthony Van Dyke, *c.* 1632–5. *(Courtesy of the National Portrait Gallery)*

as a man earns by the sweat of his brow, and no maiden ever complains, at even, of the length of the day. The issue is a fine web, which feeds the pride of the whole globe; which surrounds with its fine border cloaks and tuckers, and shows grandly round the throats and hands of Kings.

Lace and flamboyant costume were the trademarks of the Cavaliers. Antique print. *(Author's collection)*

Lace adorned everything – collars, cuffs and stocking tops – and soon became a most valuable commodity. It created a lucrative trade for the smuggler, who had been known to 'import' it into the country in objects as diverse as corsets and coffins. While the new lavish clothing styles were adopted by some, others rejected the excessive ornamentation in favour of more restrained styles. But clothing styles during the seventeenth century were not merely about looks; a person's choice of clothing also told the world about his or her religious or political positions with the Cavalier style soon associated with the Catholic religion and a strong king. Those that wished to throw off the monarchy and become a republic favoured the Roundhead cause, and in keeping with their Protestant religion dressed themselves with less flamboyance. Yet, the more circumspect in society recognised the effort it took to make lace and so allowed themselves a modicum of adornment. Not wishing to indulge in personal display did not mean those Protestants and Puritans that could afford it did not have tailors make their sober garments from rich if not ornate cloth and insist upon a fine cut and finish.

'False Face Must Hide What the False Heart Doth Know' – William Shakespeare

For more than a century women had been painting their faces in earnest and exposing themselves to the ravaging effects of lead make-up. Was it any wonder that ladies eventually turned to completely covering their faces? In 1615 a man called Edward Sharpham addressed this issue in his book *The Fleire*, with the principal character saying: 'Faith, ladies, if you used but, on mornings when you rise, the divine smoak of this celestial herb Tobacco, it will more purifie, dense, and mundifie your complexion, by ten parts, than your dissolved mercurie, your juice of lemmons, your distilled snailes, your gourd waters, your oile of tartar, or a thousand such toyes.'

Perhaps not totally convinced of the healing power of smoke, full face-masks had already arrived in England from France via Italy, where in 1570 William Harrison stated masks were first devised and used by 'curtizans' (courtesans). That may have been so but eventually masks permeated into all levels of society, with ladies of all ranks adopting them, primarily as protection. Apart from covering pox marks and other blemishes, women were concerned about their complexions when riding or out in a carriage and did not relish garnering a glow from the sun. It does seem strange to us today but in the sixteenth and seventeenth centuries it was desirable to appear pale and plump, a sign that your husband could afford for you to stay indoors and not engage in manual labour. Whereas during the twentieth and twenty-first centuries a tan has been suggestive of leisure time outdoors, previously it meant you were too poor not to work and so toiled in the fields.

Masks became an acceptable barrier to dust and grime, and gave women a way of moving about the city incognito when they were usually confined to the home, their every move judged on a moral level. Philip Stubbes in his *The Anatomie of Abuses*, written in 1583, tells us that:

When they use to ride a brod they have invisories, or visors made of velvet, wherwith they cover all their faces, having holse made in them against their eyes, whereout they look. So that if a man, that knew not their guise before, should chaunce to meet one of them, hee woould think hee met a monster or a devil, for face hee can see none, but two brode holes against her eyes with glasses in them.

There were several styles of mask, ranging from fluid fabrics such as velvet to stiff offerings consisting of an outside cover, a foundation and a lining. A reference in the *Histoire des Jouets et Jeux D'enfants* by Fournier mentions that from around 1540 a mixture of clay, paper and plaster called *carton-pierre* may have been worked together and pressed into moulds backed by coarse

Stuart-era face masks, antique print.

paper and steam dried. Literally translated *carton-pierre* means, 'stone pasteboard 'and had a papier mâché appearance, though was perhaps much heavier. Another possibility was buckram, a stiff fabric used in millinery, or pressed paper which resembled cardboard, both then being faced with fine fabric or silk and backed with 'sweet skynnes' or perfumed leather which would have been soft against the skin.

Some masks were held to the face by means of a wand or stick but this meant both hands were not free. The other way was for the women to keep the mask in place by means of a small bead threaded on a length of twisted hemp attached to the lower part of the mask which she clenched in her teeth. An ingenious way of attachment one might say, though just how a lady was supposed to talk, let alone be charmingly witty, is possibly an art lost to time. It may have rendered an otherwise chatter-filled carriage ride in the company of a bevy of ladies amusingly silent for a thankful father or husband. But it was not only gentlewomen who adhered to this quirk of fashion, it was equally indulged by royalty. When walking in her garden Elizabeth I was recorded as having 'put down her mask' to speak to a visiting merchant from Holland.

Masks may have been introduced to England in the days of Gloriana and continued to protect the complexion in the decades preceding the Restoration, but it was only when Charles II retook the English throne and reinstated the theatre that a lady's mask or 'vizard' (from the word visor) became an altogether different affair. Samuel Pepys is possibly our best source of evidence for this shift in the status of the lady's mask, its ability to evoke an air of mystery, conceal and effectively render every woman, common and highborn, equal in their anonymity. Pepys himself found masks mildly frustrating, as recorded in his diary of 1661 when he allowed his clerk and his wife a ride into town with him in his carriage. He first thought the man's wife to 'be an old woman' only to find out later, after she had removed her mask, that she was in fact 'indeed pretty'. In 1663 he recounted that 'ladies wear masks to the theatre which hides their whole face', convenient for a lady if she wished to attend incognito. Such is illustrated by an entry in which Pepys tells us how his friend Lord Falconbridge was at the 'Royall Theatre' with Lady Mary Cromwell (third daughter of Oliver Cromwell), who 'when the House began to fill she put on her vizard, and so kept it on all the play'. Unfortunately, by now the vizard was becoming a standard accessory of the prostitute who would look for custom both within the theatre and without, thus ladies in a full vizard ran the risk of appearing other than they were. Despite care being given to promote respect for the mask, Antoine de Courtin's *The Rules of Civility* (1671) advises readers to 'pay more civility' to those wearing vizards 'because many times under those disguises are persons of the highest dignity and honour', it was too little too late. Pepys recounts an incident where he and some friends were in need of a carriage after an evening out and his wife being a little ahead of him was almost 'taken up' by a gentleman who did not recognise her as she was 'wearing her vizard'.

Eventually, the word itself sank into depravity, vizard simply denoting a woman of easy virtue with theatres the places to meet them. Respectable women no longer frequented playhouses, which prompted individual premises to take action. When in 1703 the *Daily Courant* published a playbill for a performance of *The Country House* and 'a consort of musick in Drury Lane' it included a line which declared 'and no persons to be admitted in masks'. This was wholly ineffective, compelling the government to intervene with an edict issued by Queen Anne that, among other things, 'no woman be allowed or presume to wear a vizard mask in theatres'.

Beauty patches were first used to cover pox marks then were gradually adopted purely for adornment. *(Author's collection)*

Masks did not however disappear altogether as the half-mask naturally took its place. Easier for a woman to hold a conversation as she no longer needed to hold it to her face by clenching her teeth around a bead, it was also easier for her to be recognised, though it was an unwritten rule that such revelations would not be disclosed. A half-measure of facial protection and anonymity was preferable to the full mask given the effect the latter had had upon women's reputations. Did Sarah Fell of Swarthmoore Hall realise when she entered in her account book '1674 – October 17th – paid for a vizard maske for myself at 1s and 4d' that twenty years later such a devilish object would be considered to have done more to 'ruine more women's virtues than all the bawds in towne'?

Face Patches – 'Black Spots and Patches on the Face to Sober Women Bring Disgrace …'

If a woman was less inclined to embrace a half face mask it was perhaps no surprise that she naturally adopted the face patch to conceal her blemishes, smallpox scars or the ravages of potentially fatal make-up. Deadly cosmetics made it impossible for the skin to breathe and the damage inflicted was irrevocable, as one gentleman discovered to his cost on seeing his new wife the morning after the wedding. Writing as late as 1711, he recounts:

> as for my dear, never man was so enamoured as I was of her fair forehead, neck, and arms, as well as the bright jet of her hair; but to my great astonishment, I find they were all the effect of art. Her skin is so tarnished with this practice, that when she first wakes in a morning, she scarce seems young enough to be the mother of her whom I carried to bed the night

before. I shall take the liberty to part with her by the first opportunity, unless her father will make her portion suitable to her real, not her assumed countenance.

Opinions on the adoption of patching by the ladies of England also feature in John Bulwer's book *Anthropometamorphosis: Man Transform'd*, or *The Artificial Changeling*, 1650. He complains:

Our ladies, have lately entertained a vain custom of spotting their faces, out of an affectation of a mole, to set off their beauty, such as Venus had; and it is well if one black patch serves to make their faces remarkable, for some fill their visages full of them, varied unto all manner of shapes and figures.

A 'Warning to the Fair', written in 1680, states:

But fair one know your glass is run,
Your time is short, your thread is spun,
Your spotted face, and rich attire
Is fuell for eternal fire.

In truth the threat of fire and brimstone did little to deter either Cavalier or Roundhead from patching during the first half of the seventeenth century, and so Parliament, always wishing to control what it saw as the excesses of the people, introduced a bill on 7 June 1650 to deal with the 'vice of painting, wearing black patches and immodest dresses of women'. As usual, the legislation was aimed at what the government supposed was a predominantly female activity when in truth the wearing of patches was not just the prerogative of ladies.

The diarist Samuel Pepys, whose recording of everyday life in the mid-seventeenth century gives us an intimate insight into all things Stuart, mentions that his wife adopted the fashion of wearing patches of her own accord, apparently without seeking his permission. This seems strange to the modern woman who rarely, if ever, asks to be allowed to wear what she thinks suitable. Pepys, however, notes three months later that: 'my wife seemed very pretty to-day, it being the first time I had given her leave to wear a black patch'. He adds a week or so later that his wife, with two or three patches, looked far handsomer than the Princess Henrietta. Ironically, he notes in his diary that on Monday, 26 September 1664 he too succumbed to the dubious fashion, after having been unwell. He wrote: 'Up pretty well again, but my mouth very scabby, my cold being going away, so that I was forced to wear a great black patch.'

Etiquette decreed, in the words of Charles II's mistress Lady Castlemaine – whose word was law,

MAN TRANSFORMD:

OR THE

ARTIFICIALL

CHANGLING.

THE FIRST SCENE.

Certaine Fashions of the Head, affected and contrived, by the Pragmaticall invention and Artificiall endeavours of many Nations.

Ippocrates observes, that the Naturall mould or figure of the Head hath bin tampered with, and altered by Art. *Sennertus* also, where he writes,

The Artificiall Changling, written in 1653 by John Bulwer. Bulwer's aim, according to the full title, was to expose the '*mad and cruel gallantry, foolish bravery, ridiculous beauty, filthy fineness, and loathsome loveliness of most nations, fashioning & altering their bodies from the mould intended by nature*'. Bulwer describes in detail how people around the world artificially modify their appearance, noting that every nation has a 'particular whimzey as touching corporall fashions of their own invention'.

A seventeenth-century lady wearing a vizard or face mask. Antique print. *(Author's collection)*

that it was in bad taste to wear patches when in mourning but they were acceptable on the occasions of afternoons at the theatre, in the parks in the evening and in the drawing room at night. Yet, they were still ridiculed, with puritanical satirists unable to leave 'patchers' unmolested. In 1668 a poem called 'The Burse of Reformation & Wit Restored' informs us:

Heer patches are of every art
For pimples and for scarrs;
Heer's all the wandring planett signes,
And some o' th' fixed starrs,
Already gumm'd, to make them stick,
They need no other sky,
Nor starrs, for Lilly for to vew,
To tell your fortunes by.

An interesting point here is that we are privileged to discover that in some cases patches are 'ready gummed', an unusual phenomenon if it was true as generally this is only associated with the modern world. As a rule, patches were made out of velvet, silk or taffeta and attached to the face by means of a crude glue which included glycerine. If you were a woman of limited means then patches made from mouse skin had to suffice. Patches were both home-made and shop bought, purchased alongside other lady's accoutrements such as fans and hair ornaments. Their manufacture provided a sustainable piecework industry for children and older women confined to the home. So numerous were the number of patches made that they became known as 'mouchete', or 'small flies', and in Venice there is still a street called Calle de le Moschete where these fake beauty spots were produced. Joseph Addison, who co-founded the *Spectator* with his partner Richard Steele, wrote an account on the trend of 'patching' after visiting an opera in Haymarket. With the seventeenth century only just having given way to the first years of the ever political eighteenth, his observations make delightful reading. He did, however, warn in the *Spectator* on Saturday, 2 June 1711 that:

This account of Party Patches will, I'm afraid appear improbable to those who live at a distance from the fashionable world.

About the Middle of last Winter I went to see an Opera at the Theatre in the Hay-Market, where I could not but take notice of two Parties of very fine Women, that had placed themselves in the opposite Side-Boxes, and seemed drawn up in a kind of Battle-Array one against another. After a short Survey of them, I found they were Patch'd differently; the Faces on one Hand, being spotted on the right Side of the Forehead, and those upon the other on the Left. I quickly perceived that they cast hostile Glances upon one another and that their Patches were placed in those different Situations, as Party-Signals to distinguish Friends from Foes. In the Middle-Boxes, between these two opposite bodies, were several Ladies who Patched indifferently on both Sides of their Faces, and seem'd to sit there with no other Intention but to see the Opera. Upon Inquiry I found, that the Body of Amazons on my Right Hand, were Whigs, and those on my Left, Tories: And that those who had placed themselves in the Middle Boxes were a Neutral Party, whose Faces had not yet declared themselves. These last, however, as I afterwards found, diminished daily, and took their Party with one Side

Patches had secret meanings depending where they were placed on the face. *(Author's collection)*

or the other; insomuch that I observed in several of them, the Patches, which were before dispersed equally, are now all gone over to the Whig or Tory Side of the Face. The Censorious say, That the Men, whose hearts are aimed at, are very often the Occasions that one Part of the Face is thus dishonoured, and lies under a kind of Disgrace, while the other is so much Set off and Adorned by the Owner; and that the Patches turn to the Right or to the Left, according to the Principles of the Man who is most in Favour. But whatever may be the Motives of a few fantastical Coquets, who do not Patch for the Publick Good so much as for their own private Advantage, it is certain, that there are several Women of Honour who patch out of Principle, and with an Eye to the Interest of their Country. Nay, I am informed that some of them adhere so stedfastly to their Party, and are so far from sacrificing their Zeal for the Publick to their Passion for any particular Person, that in a late Draught of Marriage-Articles a Lady has stipulated with her Husband, That, whatever his Opinions are, she shall be at liberty to Patch on which Side she pleases.

I must here take notice, that Rosalinda, a famous Whig Partizan, has most unfortunately a very beautiful Mole on the Tory Part of her Forehead; which being very conspicuous, has occasioned many Mistakes, and given an Handle to her Enemies to misrepresent her Face, as tho' it had Revolted from the Whig Interest. But, whatever this natural Patch may seem to intimate, it is well known that her Notions of Government are still the same. This unlucky Mole, however, has mis-led several Coxcombs; and like the hanging out of false Colours, made some of them converse with Rosalinda in what they thought the Spirit of her Party, when on a sudden she has given them an unexpected Fire, that has sunk them all at once. If Rosalinda is unfortunate in her Mole, Nigranilla is as unhappy in a Pimple, which forces her, against her Inclinations, to Patch on the Whig Side.

I am told that many virtuous Matrons, who formerly have been taught to believe that this artificial Spotting of the Face was unlawful, are now reconciled by a Zeal for their Cause, to what they could not be prompted by a Concern for their Beauty. This way of declaring War upon one another, puts me in mind of what is reported of the Tigress, that several Spots rise in her Skin when she is angry, or as Mr. Cowley has imitated the Verses that stand as the Motto on this Paper, '… She swells with angry Pride, And calls forth all her spots on ev'ry side.

As well as declaring political loyalty, a more discreet code also developed as a means of communication between lovers. Books were written on the art of patching, full of instructions as to where to position a patch to convey a precise message. While a patch near the eye indicated passion, one by the mouth showed boldness. A married woman could wear a spot on her right cheek whereas if she were only engaged it would have to be placed on the left.

A beauty spot on the corner of the eye indicated passion, while one near the eyes suggested irresistibility. Other beauty spot meanings included: on the throat – gallantry; on the nose – boldness or shamelessness; in the middle of the forehead – dignified; and the middle of the cheek – bold; touching the edge of lower lip – discreet; near the corner of the eye – available; and one beside the mouth – a tantalising 'I will kiss but go no further'.

The need for patches led to an equally lucrative trade in patch boxes, which were cheap and convenient presents for young girls and women to give to each other. Equally, a small box inscribed with a secret message could be given as a clandestine gift between lovers

Patches continued well into the Georgian era, only really going out of fashion in the Regency period, but there was always concern about a woman's obsession with the 'patch'. A wonderful piece in the *Ipswich Journal*, dated 1774, illustrates this concern, which had been present from the inception of the fad. A certain gentleman named Sir Kenelm Digby was in no way enamoured of women's beauty patches, thinking them quite unnecessary; vulgar in fact, stating that should they have occurred naturally on a woman's face they would be deemed a deformity. He could not understand why a woman with an unblemished countenance should wish to deform herself so? To illustrate his dislike he recounted a tale of a relation of his, a niece who being a stunning natural beauty paid him a visit one day her face sporting several patches on her otherwise flawless countenance. Sir Kenelm argued with her hoping to dissuade her from the use of such ornaments citing the fact that as she was pregnant at the time no good could come of it. 'Have you no apprehension that your child may be born with half-moons upon his face; or rather, that all the black which you spot in several places, up and down, may assemble in one, and appear in the middle of his forehead?' This did in fact prompt her to stop using patches, his words having such a influence on her imagination that when she was delivered of a daughter who was born with a spot 'as large as a crown of gold in the middle of her forehead' she blamed herself for the unfortunate deformity unreservedly.

The Fan – Provider of Privacy, Mystery and Allure

Just as there was a potential secret language inherent in where a face patch was placed, so too the fan was an instrument both of practicality and intrigue. Itself an object of mystery constructed from 'leaves', 'rivets', 'ribs', 'sticks', 'slips' and 'guardsticks', this moveable work of art was undoubtedly a most important accessory for a wealthy woman in the seventeenth century. Huge quantities of fans were imported into Europe from China by the East India Company from the seventeenth century onwards. For years fixed or paddle fans had been the norm, mostly consisting of feathers set into ornate handles. Indeed, Queen Elizabeth I of England declared that 'the only worthy gift of a queen are fans', though this could well have originated from the queen having been told that she had very beautiful hands, and holding a fan would emphasise such beauty. But later it was the folding fan which became a status symbol, the rich able to afford exquisite examples of silk stretched between handles of ivory, carved wood or even gold studded with jewels. The French especially loved the fan and one belonging to Madame de Pompadour, mistress of Louis XV, included paper that was cut in imitation of lace, contained ten painted miniatures, took nine years to make and cost almost £20,000. Artists that decorated fans were not averse to signing them as they would a painting, as some were indeed works of art.

As the fan eventually filtered down to women at all levels of society it was clear its popularity lay not so much in its stunning craftsmanship as in its ability, when correctly handled, to speak volumes in a world which generally allowed women few words.

Just as newspaper proprietor Joseph Addison had lampooned patches in his *Spectator*, he also wrote a satirical piece on women's adoration of the fan. He decries that 'Women are armed with fans as men with swords, and sometimes do more execution with them.' He alludes to the many ways a fan can be unfurled, slowly and deliberately with many different flicks of the wrist, each denoting a myriad of different emotions. Similarly, the means by which a fan was closed, sometimes with 'a crack like a pocket-pistol', could show just what humour a woman was in. He finishes with describing the infinite ways a fan can be fluttered:

There is an infinite variety of motions to be made use of in the flutter of a fan. There is the angry flutter, the modest flutter, the timorous flutter, the confused flutter, the merry flutter, and the amorous flutter. Not to be tedious, there is scarce any emotion in the mind which does not produce a suitable agitation in the fan; insomuch, that if I only see the fan of a disciplined lady, I know very well if she laughs, frowns, or blushes. I have seen a fan so very angry, that it would have been dangerous for the absent lover who provoked it to have come within wind of it; and at other times so very languishing, that I have been glad for the

'Women are armed with fans as men with swords, and sometimes do more execution with them', *Spectator*, 1711.

Lady with the Veil, Alexander Roslin, 1768.

lady's sake the lover was at a sufficient distance from it. I need not add, that a fan is either a prude or a coquette, according to the nature of the person that bears it.

The observation that 'ladies have but little talk and the main conversation is the flutter of the fans' was both true and naïve. In fact, ladies well versed in the art of the fan were speaking a most clandestine language which could see a lady communicate across a room without saying a word. Unfortunately, men wishing to enter into a relationship with any female of the time would also have to observe the rules closely. There were more than a dozen basic fan-related gestures that a man would need to know, for example:

Touching right cheek – yes
Touching left cheek – no
Twirling in right hand – I love another
Fanning slowly – I am married
Fanning quickly – I am engaged
Open and shut – you are cruel
Open wide – wait for me
Presented shut – do you love me?
With handle to lip – Kiss me
In right hand in front of face – Follow me
Drawing across the cheek – I love you
Placing on left ear – I wish to get rid of you

For an interested beau it must have been a minefield as variations on the themes also applied. If a lady appeared upon her balcony, slowly fanning herself, before returning inside and closing the windows after her it meant 'I cannot go out'. If she did the same but fanned herself excitedly and left the windows open, it meant that she'd be out soon. Slow fanning on its own meant 'Don't waste your time I do not care for you', while fanning at speed denoted 'I love you so much'. Carrying the fan closed and hanging from her left hand meant the lady was engaged, but if hanging from her right meant the opposite and she was wishing she was so. If she dropped her fan the gentleman may deduce that she 'belongs to him', while a half-open fan over a woman's face warned of being watched.

CHAPTER 6

Gorgeous Georgians

'False rumps – false teeth – false hair – false faces –
Alas! Poor man how hard thy case is;
Instead of 'woman, heav'nly woman's charms,
To clasp cork – gum – wool – varnish – in thy arms.'
Epigram entitled 'Man's Misfortune', *Hampshire Chronicle*, 1777

There was no ignoring aristocratic ladies''high-hair' during the Georgian era. Women fainted from the weight of additional wigs and decorations, ducked under doors to avoid collisions and sat on the floors of coaches due to the scale of it. Many employed 2lb of whitening powder per 'dressing' simply to maintain their extravagant styles.

The epitome of an 'age of elegance', an elaborate hairstyle was of course just another dazzling and impractical creation, along with wide skirts and beauty patches, which became de rigueur for members of aristocratic society.

There were no end of contraptions and contrivances on the market aimed at contorting the symmetry of the human form into a parody of itself. The eighteenth century was an age where nothing was as it seemed and gentleman protested that they preferred their women to be, if nothing else, at least real. Upper class men were concerned that beneath a woman's powder and wigs they didn't really know what their wives and sweethearts looked like or whether they would recognise them without it? A poem in the *Lady's Magazine* of 1777 seems to hit the nail right on the head:

Give Chloe a bushel of horsehair and wool
Of paste and pomatum a pound
Ten yards of gay ribbon to deck her sweet scull
And gauze to encompass it round.
Let her gown be tucked up to the hip on each side
Shoes too high for to walk or to jump
And to deck the sweet charmer complete for a bride
Let the cork cutter make her a rump
Thus finished in taste while on Chloe you gaze
you may take the dear charmer for life
but never undress her, for out of her stays
You'll find you have lost half your wife.

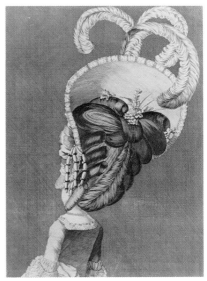

A 1776 print entitled *OH-HEIGH-OH* showing an elaborate hairstyle full of twists and curls. If not a wig then false hair would have been used to create such a gravity defying style with sugar water employed to add volume. *(Library of Congress)*

Georgiana Cavendish, Duchess of Devonshire (1757–1806). *(Author's collection)*

A Pig in a Poke by James Phillips, 1786. This before and after cartoon illustrates how by donning a false rump, wig and petticoats the Georgian woman's figure was exaggerated. *(Library of Congress)*

The Georgian woman in all her incarnations was a creature of pretence. That is not to say that gentlemen did not also indulge in padding and disguise, but it was in female dress that we see the greatest deceptions. By deconstructing the frivolous sentiments of the poem quoted on p. 55 it is possible to unravel the layers that made up the Georgian beauty.

Hair: Pigtails, Pomatum and Periwigs

It was never the aim of the upper class Georgians to look natural. To be 'styled,' was paramount and this extended not only to dress but to taste and manners. Dressed hair was 'polite hair' in civilised Georgian society. Hair was elaborate and necessitated extensions – 'top pieces' for crowns, 'borders' for the front, 'curls, neck braids and chignons' of various lengths for the back. If that wasn't enough, feathers, jewels and fabrics were often added. A satirical entry in the *Gentleman's Magazine* of 1773 commented: 'such bushes of hair as the ladies bore upon their heads in the last and present year so enormous that they seem to require a gardener's sheers instead of scissors, to reduce them to tolerable dimensions!' Satire aside, there was a thriving market for human hair and hair merchants sourced the best quality both from England and abroad. As hairdresser James Stewart observed in 1782, hair 'was a considerable article in commerce' and sold that year for between 5 shillings and £5 per ounce (dependent on quality). The most sought after hair was that from a healthy virgin. Hair supplies from abroad were quarantined for fear of it bringing plague or other terrible diseases into the country, and if there was a shortage then at the other end of the financial scale cheap wigs were available, made of horsehair and wool which made them extremely uncomfortable.

Eventually gendered and popular with both sexes, wigs were originally used to cover thinning or general hair loss, with high-profile women such as Queen Elizabeth I and Mary Queen of Scots owning a collection of different styles. However, the majority of wigs were first worn by men.

The word 'wig' came into the English vocabulary by a strange evolution. Starting in Rome, the word *pilus* travelled to Spain where it became *pelo* and *peluca*. In France the word changed to *perruque* and in Holland to *peruic*. Coming to England from the Low Countries, it became 'perwick', 'perwig', 'periwig' and finally was shortened to 'wig'.

During the English Civil War (1642–51) there was no time for wigs. Hair tended to be a man's own but on the Restoration of the monarchy there was a wig upon every fashionable Englishman's head, King Charles II himself having adopted the full-bottomed wig, a style that exaggerated his 'majesty' and commanded respect. By its very construction of row upon row of curls reaching to the chest, it proved to be extremely expensive, costing between 30 and 40 guineas, and fading from fashion by the 1720s. The tradition was continued by the legal profession, ecclesiastical dignitaries and of course doctors, of whom the public, according to Fielding's farce, *The Mock Doctor*, 'would put the least confidence in a physician who wore his own hair'.

Other types of wigs, however, were more affordable, but seen as no less important. In his treatise on hairdressing entitled *Plocarosmos, or The Whole Art of Hairdressing* (1782), James Stewart concluded, 'all conditions of men were distinguished by the cut of his wig'. Thus, there was a wig to suit any office in life.

Tie wigs caught the hair at the back of the neck and held it with a bow, and were the most popular type and formed the basis of many other styles. Pigtail wigs, for example, consisted of

A barber and wigmaker's shop from Diderot's *Encyclopédie, ou dictionnaire raisonné des sciences, des arts et des métiers*, c. 1751. *(Author's collection)*

either one, two or three lengths of hair tightly wrapped in a spiral manner with black silk ribbons. They were tied at the nape of the neck with a ribbon bow. It was a fashion particularly popular during the reign of George II and very expensive. The Mildmay Papers held at the Essex Record Office suggest that in 1734 the price of 'a tied wig' was over £7.

Good quality wigs were targets for thieves with wigs even being whipped off men's heads in broad daylight. Entries in the *Newgate Calendar* bear witness to just how serious an offence this was perceived to be. On 8 March 1698 Edward Short of St Martin-in the-Fields was indicted for robbing Peter Newell of a hat and 'periwig'. Charged with violent highway robbery, the accused received the death penalty. John Corbet of the parish of St Faith's, London was likewise condemned for 'violently taking from James Shippard, upon the Queens Highway, a peruke'. George Hayns of St Giles-in-the-Fields was convicted of stealing a 'periwig from Jacob Coler in Drury Lane' in 1717. All were executed.

The 'bag' wig was not only fashionable but convenient. A square or rectangular bag was drawn tight about the end of the hair with a bow and a drawstring and protected the coat from grease and powder. However, by the 1740s the bag was often so large that it practically covered the shoulders of the wearer. A useful sideline from this particular fashion was that impoverished men and women could earn a meagre living from making such bags.

The Ramillies was essentially a military wig, thought to take its name from the battle of that name that was fought between the French and the English in 1706, during which in order to free themselves from their cumbersome full-bottomed wigs soldiers plaited the hair into long queues called 'Ramillie-tails'. These were tied and fastened with a large bow at the nape of the neck, and a smaller one at the end. It was a style favoured by younger men and it was thought to imbue them with a military air as the wig became standard dress for the British Army. Read's *Weekly Journal* of 1 May 1736, in a report on the marriage of the Prince of Wales, stated that 'the officers of the Horse and Foot Guards wore Ramillie periwigs by His Majesty's order'.

The rise and fall of the male periwig was phenomenal with styles including the 'Campaign' or 'Travelling' wig, the 'Bob', both 'long', 'short' and 'snug', the Caxton, Toupee and Foretop, the Spencer, the Adonis, the 'Natty Scratch', a sports, riding and business wig, as well as those that were 'frizzed' and 'grizzled' and the plain 'Cut Wig', mainly worn by artisans. Wigs found favour with parsons and in the course of time they became indispensable, even warranting recommendation. In 1756 a volume was issued under the title of *Free Advice to a Young Clergyman*, written by the Revd John Chubbe, in which he advised the young preacher always to wear a full wig until age had made his own hair respectable. Wigs even made it on to the second-hand market, re-shaped and re-dressed to the best of a hairdresser's ability.

Sir Richard Haddock (1629–1714), Admiral of the Royal Navy, wearing a 'full-bottomed' style of wig. *(Author's collection)*

But nothing was to prove as popular as the 'high hair' adopted by ladies when, in 1770, wigs became fashionable among women too. Taller, more sophisticated and not to mention preposterous, they were to overtake the trend that had seen men both shave their heads and disguise their natural hair.

As the demand for male wigs had been waning, in the 1760s suppliers found their livelihoods in jeopardy. Out of necessity, in 1765 wigmakers petitioned King George III to grant them relief 'in consideration of their distressed condition occasioned by so many people wearing their own hair'. The answer was for wigmakers, who had gradually evolved from simple barbers, to now re-emerge as hairdressers, catering for the puffs, rolls, pigtails and bags which continued to be used in much the same manner as before. If you were, however, practised in the art of applying powder and pomatum, you would always be indispensable to both sexes.

No more than animal fat, pomatum

A bag wig.

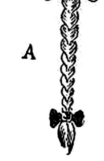

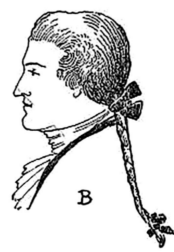

A   B   C

Ramillies wig.

Des Victoire Coiffure a la Grenade, 1779. (Library of Congress)

needed to be perfumed to achieve a sweet smell, and in order to have a clear cream appearance and light texture the grease ideally had to be taken from a young and healthy animal. Powder, on the other hand, a product that had been in use from the early 1700s, was obtained from many sources and was easily corrupted. Standards did apply but as a gentleman's wig or hair required only black, white, brown or grey colouring they were easier to adhere to. At the other end of the scale, ladies had a penchant for pastel colours, namely pink, light violet or blue and so pigments added could mask a bad product.

Whereas the best hair powders consisted of starch from corn, wheat, rice and occasionally potato, cheaper powders were made up of flour, alabaster, plaster of Paris, whiting and lime. Despite the law decreeing hair powder had to contain starch, many ignored it. According to the *Newcastle Courant*, dated 1739, 'On Tuesday about 20 peruke-makers were convicted at the Excise-Office for using and having in their custody Hair-Powder not made of starch.' On 20 October 1745, it was recorded that fifty-one barbers in England were convicted before the commissioners of excise, and fined a penalty of £20, contrary to an Act of Parliament, as were forty-nine others in the same month.

As ladies' hair creations grew so did the demand for the powder that coated the sculpting pomatum and fixed the style. Powder was applied in a small room designed for the purpose (and the upwardly mobile) with the client cloaked in a powdering garment, sitting in a chair. As he/she then protected the face and eyes with a paper mask or funnel-shaped 'nosebag', the barber, using a bellows or large powder-puff, enveloped his client's head in powder. It was said that you could judge a lady's intellect, if not her common sense, by the powder in her wig. No less extraordinary was a young man seen leaving a barber's shop, 'his wig containing a pound of hair but with two pounds of powder in it', as recorded in a contemporary newspaper. The importance of a well-powdered head was reiterated by a young man who wrote in a periodical paper in 1751, 'my mother would rather follow me to my grave than see me sneak about with dirty shoes and blotted fingers, hair unpowdered, and a hat uncocked …'.

Wigs were convenient to maintain as one could send them back to the barbers for re-dressing at regular intervals. The alternative was having to sit while your hair was combed, pulled, frizzed, teased, rearranged about pads of greasy wool and pinned, pomaded, pummelled and powdered into shape. Yet the dressing of the hair was only half of the process. The other half was just 'wearing' your new hairstyle, day and night, for an average of three or four weeks, and in some cases even sleeping sitting up to preserve it. Only after time would the creation be pulled down and rebuilt. Even if a lady could have afforded the expense of a daily change in order to prevent the animal grease in the pomatum becoming rancid and attracting bugs or at worst nests of mice, it is unlikely she would have wanted to spend hours in the hairdresser's chair.

A wonderful extract from the *London Magazine* of 1768 gives us a first-hand account of such activities:

> I went the other morning to make a visit to an elderly aunt of mine,
> when I found her pulling off her cap and tendering her head to the
> ingenious Mr. Gilchrist, who had lately obliged the public with a
> most excellent essay on hair. He asked her how long it was since
> her head had been opened or repaired. She answered, 'Not above
> nine weeks.' To which he replied it was as long as a head could
> well go in the summer, and that therefore it was proper to deliver
> it now: for he confessed that it began to be un peu hazardie.

The discomfort ladies must have felt from their elaborate hairstyles was addressed by the introduction of head-scratchers, which, used in open company, were made from either bone, ivory, silver or gold depending on means.

Aside from physical discomfort, sporting high hair was fraught with other problems. Poet Samuel Rogers (1763–1855) recollected in his youth that ladies' dressed hair 'was of a truly preposterous size'. On one occasion he was obliged to share a coach with a lady who had to sit on a stool placed at the bottom of the coach as the height of her headdress did not allow her to sit on the seat! How battered and bruised she must have felt once she had spilled out of the coach is anyone's guess. Dancing was no easier as ladies with high hair could not pass under the raised arms of their gentleman partners. It is also rumoured that a side door in St Paul's cathedral had to be raised at least 4ft just to enable women to enter the building.

It wasn't always the hair that confounded matters, as hair ornaments also posed a danger to the wearer. When the Duchess of Devonshire introduced feathers a yard high into her coiffeur there was public outcry. She was branded 'immoral' and ladies who did likewise were denounced from the pulpit, insulted, mobbed and persecuted. Candle-lit chandeliers were also a hazard as hair could catch fire when a lady passed under it unaware of the danger until it was too late.

In the last decade of the eighteenth century the whole phenomenon of enormous wigs and powdered hair was becoming a contentious subject. On 16 January 1790 one gentleman writing in the *Norfolk Chronicle* considered, as wheat was in short supply and the country engaged in corn and bread riots, whether it was wise to use the precious commodity for the hair instead of putting it into the mouths of the hungry? To the best of his ability he attempted to calculate just how much flour was used for the 'unnecessary' upkeep of the nation's heads. He assumed that out of 40,000 inhabitants there were on average 5 to a family, resulting in 8,000 families, a number he then halved because due to their 'situation in life' they could not be 'supposed to use powder'. He then absolved a further 2,000 families for being only occasional users and so consequently having a 'trifling effect' on the equation, settling on the remaining 2,000. Of these he reckoned 3 individuals in every 2 families were in 'constant use of it', having their hair or wigs dressed daily with powder.

A gentleman 'with a queue' in four dressings consumes 1lb. of powder – the ladies much more; it will therefore be making a full allowance for those who dress more lightly to calculate the consumption of each individual at half a pound weekly or 1,500 lb. altogether. As much wheat is consumed in the manufacture of 1lb of flour, there being as much waste attending the process of making starch, which is powder unground, as of grinding of wheat into flour. One lb. of flour will make 1lb 5oz of bread and as 6 lb. of bread will supply an individual for a week, 5lb of flour will be more than sufficient; 1,500lb which is used in hair powder will then be found adequate to the support of 300 persons – a fact so striking it needs no comment.

The Flower Garden, hand-coloured etched engraving published by M. Darly in 1777. *(Library of Congress)*

The writer states that he has not in any way exaggerated his findings and calls on his fellow citizens to 'refuse to still the cries of only one poor infant, to indulge in the paltry gratification of a powdered head'.

Powder was still used up until 1793 when ladies finally abandoned it taking their lead from Queen Charlotte, wife of George III. The French Revolution also effected a change as in France a powdered head or wig was a sign of aristocracy and a sure route to the guillotine. In England on 5 May 1795 a tax on hair powder was introduced in an attempt to end the practice. The Duty on Hair Powder Act was passed by Parliament and not repealed until 1869.

To the modern eye the tax appears amusing. Everyone wishing to use hair powder had to visit a stamp office to enter their name and pay for an annual certificate costing 1 guinea. As with any dictate, there were certain exemptions, the most obvious being the royal family and their servants, as well as clergymen with an income of under £100 a year, but the tax did eventually have the desired effect.

'Lucy Locket Lost her Pocket ...'

From the seventeenth to the late nineteenth centuries most women had at least one pair of pockets, which served a similar purpose to the handbag today. Unlike a handbag, however, pockets were rarely if ever seen as they were usually worn underneath the skirt, usually tied around the waist under a lady's petticoats. To access her pockets a woman simply had to slip her hands into slits in the side seams of her gown and into the opening of the pocket. Men didn't wear separate pockets, as theirs were sewn into the linings of their coats, waistcoats and breeches.

Many pockets were handmade and they were often given as gifts. Some were made to match a petticoat or waistcoat, while some were made over from old clothes or textiles. Pockets could also be bought ready-made from a haberdasher.

Women kept a wide variety of objects in their pockets. In the days when people often shared bedrooms and household furniture, a pocket was sometimes the only private, safe place for small personal possessions.

'Lucy Locket Lost Her Pocket' is a well-known nursery rhyme, though totally unsuitable for the nursery. Its adult message is one of taking care with what you wish for – rival mistresses Kitty Fisher and Lucy Locket and references to Cassanova and Charles II – while also illustrating that from the lowliest of women to ladies and queens pockets were an indispensable part of a woman's life. However, being detachable, like Tudor sleeves two centuries before, they could be lost or even worse stolen. The Old Bailey records tell us that thieves known as 'pickpockets' used a variety of methods to snatch pockets such as cutting the pocket strings and grabbing the pocket or slashing the pocket itself so the contents fell out.

'On 5 November 1716 Robert Draw of London, labourer, was indicted for privately stealing from Martha Peacock a linen Pocket (value 2 shillings) complete with contents', as recorded in Proceedings of the Old Bailey. Martha told the authorities that she had been going along the street when the prisoner had come up behind her, thrust his hand up her riding-hood and pulled her pocket off. She said she had cried out causing a chase to take place. Eventually knocked down, the accused was found to have the pocket upon him. Though found guilty to the value of 10 pence, he vehemently denied the charge. William Carlisle was also brought before the Old Bailey Courthouse, where on 4 December 1717 he was duly charged with privately stealing a 'Pocket, value 1 pence; 2 Gold Rings, value 19 shillings, … a Laced Handkerchief, value 10 shillings and 2 shillings 6 pence in Money, from the Person of Susan Wright'. The assault had been an embarrassing one as Carlisle 'with great violence' had pulled off the pocket inadvertently, tearing down her petticoat in the process of doing so. The woman in a state of undress was not able to give chase, though she believed the boy who had eventually been apprehended was the culprit. Lack of evidence resulted in the lad being acquitted.

Pickpockets answered to a variety of names, as one poor woman standing in St Bartholomew's fair with a child in her arms discovered in 1729. A 'sharper' cut a hole in her pocket so dextrously that

Pockets were completely separate from any garment and reached via discreet openings in the side of a woman's skirts and petticoats. *(Photograph Tessa Hallmann)*

he got away with 20 shillings and a gold ring of the same value. Covent Garden Playhouses were another lucrative venue for the pickpocket where booty was pawned almost as fast as it was stolen with Grays Inn Lane becoming the place one lady was knocked down by two fellows who proceeded to cut off her pockets and rob her of her satin cloak, 'a muff and bonnet'. If transportation was not a thief's fate then the gallows certainly were, as Sarah Kingman found out after she had picked the pocket of Moses Wheeler in 1739.

In order to secure one's pockets during the night it was common practice to put them under your pillow, but it was no cast-iron solution. Even empty pockets were valuable and stolen along with other garments as all items of clothing were liable to theft as they could easily be pawned. Advertisements for stolen goods often appeared in newspapers. After having two pairs of pockets stolen in January 1772 along with tablecloths, shifts, stockings, aprons, gloves, a dresser cloth and a silver spoon, a gentleman in Fulham, London posted in the *Public Advertiser* that if anyone witnessed the items being offered up to be pawned or sold, they should stop them and 'give notice to Sir John Fielding whereby you shall receive five guineas reward on conviction of the offenders'.

Before James Dalton, the notorious 'captain' of a street robbery gang operating in the Smithfield area of London, was finally hanged at Tyburn in 1730, he reputedly revealed the safest way for a lady to wear her pockets, given that from childhood he had become an expert in removing them. Explaining that pickpockets could easily 'whip hold of' a pocket when worn under hoop petticoats, he went on to advise that they should instead tie them between their hoops and upper petticoats so that they might defy all the thieves in London.

In the closing decade of the eighteenth century fashions changed dramatically and the wide hoops and full petticoats that could hide a pocket went out of style. New high waistlines and a slender silhouette prompted a change in the way a woman secured her personal belongings. It was now that the forerunner of the handbag took shape. Called a reticule, it was designed to be worn on the arm and would soon become an indispensable female accessory. For many it could not replace the roomy secret of the pocket and in some cases, among the less fashionable, pockets continued to be worn. In 1819 Theresa Tidy wrote a small guide for young

A pickpocket/cutpurse at work, from the *Lottery Contrast*, 1760, by an unknown artist. *(Library of Congress)*

women entitled *Eighteen Maxims of Neatness and Order* in which she points out the manners best acquired by a gentlewoman. It is evident that even two decades after their apparent demise she still advocates the use of the pocket as she advises most strongly, 'Never sally forth from your own room in the morning without that old-fashioned article of dress – a pocket. Discard forever that modern invention called a ridicule (properly reticule).'

It is a well-known adage that what goes up must eventually come down, and an 'Essay on Fashion' featured in *Town and Country* magazine of 1787 reiterated such in no uncertain terms. Looking back over recent years, the article informed its readers that the towering and pompous ladies headdresses of the last few seasons alone could have filled an entire volume. It then pointed out that recently 'what women had taken from their heads, they have added to their hips', closing finally with relief that now the enormous hoops and large high hair had at last 'sunk under their own weight' the way was left clear for 'false rumps to be in vogue'.

It is doubtful that the modern woman – to whom comfortable clothes and ease of movement are paramount, could appreciate just how radical a change these new 'false' or 'cork' rumps were for her ancestor. Our distant grandmothers were about to be released from the tyranny of the infernal 'hoop', which like the farthingale before and the crinoline after would ensure a woman would not go unnoticed, 'so much are they persuaded that their merit be in proportion to the space they occupy in the world' as a contemporary newspaper reported.

It is hard to imagine what it must have been like to be dominated by a hoop whether full, half or basket-like, not to mention the names that had to be remembered. Such was the tyranny of the 'cage' that old French hoops had identities, for example, the 'Gourgandine', or the flirting hoop, the 'Tatez-y', or 'groping hoop', or the 'Ceillrite', otherwise known as the 'flying top-over- tail hoop'. Perhaps the latter was partly to blame for the incident reported in the *Derby Mercury* on Friday, 7 December 1748:

> Last night the ball at St James was very brilliant, their royal hignesses the prince and princess of Wales opened it, and afterwards Prince George and Princess Augusta danced. An accident happened at the ball which put two ladies into a great confusion; one of them going to take her seat by the other, in taking up the side of her hoop happened, by accident to fling it over her head, which caught hold of a sprig of diamonds and could not be disentangled for some time which however ended with no other bad consequences than much disordering the ladies head and occasioning some mirth to the noble audience.

Perhaps the most recognisable eighteenth-century underskirt construction was the pannier, which took its name from the French for 'basket'. This could either be a huge full-petticoat contraption which set its wearer out into the world like a galleon in full sail, or shorter 'side-panniers' which sat over each hip and were marginally more comfortable but had a woman resemble a pack horse. Often these small baskets were able to collapse up on themselves and so render a woman more manoeuvrable. Whichever was preferred, both dominated the middle part of the eighteenth century and are instantly recognisable as the undergarment that gave a woman her unique 'oblong' silhouette. Flat to the front and back, this wide shape was a favourite at court, in fact ordered to be worn by Queen Charlotte, wife of George III, as it was the best way to exhibit exquisite gowns. The width of panniers was varied. Some were modest while others could extend out from the waist up to 4ft on either side.

The absurdity of this fashion attracted biting social comment and many caricaturists poked fun at the women who wore them. In 1741 a contributor to the *London Magazine* noted, 'I have been in a moderate large Room, where there have been but two Ladies, who had not enough space to move without lifting up their Petticoats higher than their Grandmother's would have thought decent.' Not only were these skirts absurd but also nowhere near lightweight. Materials used included cane,

A complete Georgian gown. *(Photograph Tessa Hallmann)*   Georgian side-panniers. *(Photograph Tessa Hallmann)*

wood, whalebone or reeds and were at best inconvenient as if a lady did not choose to rest her arms upon her skirts, she would experience back ache. In addition, one had to learn *how* to wear them. No lady could simply don a hoop and know how to manoeuvre herself either indoors or out.

Doorways were a particular hazard. As some panniers were designed to collapse up upon themselves it was possible for a lady to pull her skirt up and in at the sides thus reducing her width. If this was not possible she simply had to negotiate a doorway by going through it sideways. Chairs could only be sat on if they were without armrests, while carriages had to be entered carefully, often with a footman pushing from behind. Such was mentioned in the *London Magazine* of 1741, where it applauded how a lady might get 'in and out of the narrow limits of a chair or chariot ever so skilfully or modestly, yet she makes a very odd grotesque figure with her petticoats standing up halfway up the glasses [windows] and her head peeping out above them'. Women often became entangled in other women's skirts and if taking a gentleman's arm the man in question would have to walk slightly in front of his female companion to accommodate the amount of space she occupied. Dancing was by no means an intimate affair as all movement was obliged to be undertaken at arm's length.

Fortunately, salvation was on the way in the guise of the false or cork rump, releasing women from twenty years of being 'oblong' to once more becoming rounder. It was in effect a 'bustle' before the Victorians had invented the concept and were pads filled with fabric or cork, tied at the waist and draped over the derrière, 'poofing' out the skirt at the back. As with all things the

An antique print of 1875 depicting dress in the eighteenth century named *Modes des Femmes*. *(Author's collection)*

fashion lead to a flood of satire and derision. 'Bum-shops' sprang up all over London, encouraging ladies of all incomes to 'get your false bums here'. It only added to gentlemen's confusion as to what real women looked like.

Cork rumps were popular enough to see bewildered husbands and fiancés write to newspapers and broadsheets for help, such as the 1776 December issue of the *Weekly Miscellany*:

A most ingenious author has made it a question, whether a man marrying a woman may not lawfully sue for divorce on the grounds that she is not the same person? What with the enormous false head-dress – painting – and this new-fangled cork substitute – it would be almost impossible for a man to know his bride the morning of his nuptials. If the ladies look on this invention as an ornament to their symmetry, I will engage they shall be excelled by almost any Dutch market-woman or fat landlady in this kingdom.

A cartoon by Matthew Darly from 1777 entitled 'Chloe's Cushion or The Cork Rump' epitomises the fervour for the appendage though wearing it could be hazardous. During a riot which broke out during an election at Westminster in 1784 the Guards were called and the crowd fired upon. Two ladies lost portions of their wigs, several were 'deprived of their eye-brows' and one woman had her cork rump shot off.

Like all outrageous fashion, such excesses were ridiculed and portrayed in cartoons to humiliating effect. One caricature with the titillating title 'The Bum-Bailiff outwitted, or the convenience of Fashion' (1786) is a case in point, as well as epitomising the 'false' culture of Georgian society. According to Francis Grose's *Dictionary of the Vulgar Tongue* (1811), a bum bailiff was a sheriff's officer who arrested debtors, no doubt alluding to the fact such debt

THE BUM SHOP.

The Bum Shop. (Library of Congress)

collectors were always at a debtor's back. At first glance it is easy to sympathise with the young lady portrayed in the clutches of the collector even if it is she who has run up an alarming debt by literally 'buying into' the trend that saw women wish to appear something they were not. But then the financial ruin brought about by investing in a frizzed wig, over-sized hat and false rump actually provides her with an escape. As the bailiff seizes her, warrant in hand, she slips free in her shift, leaving him holding her empty finery instead of her person. The caption reads:

> Suky like Syrinx changes shape,
> Her vain pursuer to escape:
> Ye Snapps, of Pan's hard fate beware,
> Who thought his arms embraced the fair
> But found an empty Bum-case there.

Eventually, the cork rump faded in popularity, replaced by the Grecian silhouette and the Empire gowns of the Regency. It was probably the only time from the sixteenth to nineteenth centuries that a woman's hips were not encased in whalebone, padded with cork or engulfed in horsehair!

The Bum-Bailiff outwitted, or, the convenience of Fashion, published 6 May 1786 by S.W. Fores, at the Caracature Warehouse, Piccadilly. *(Library of Congress)*

The Honourable TOM DASHALL and his cousin BOB in the lobby at Drury lane theatre, an etching by G. Cruikshank, *Illustrated London News*, c. 1821. *(Author's collection)*

CHAPTER 7

False Calves and Rising Moons

'If people turn to look at you in the street, you are not well dressed, but either too stiff, too tight, or too fashionable.'

Beau Brummell

Famed for its high hair and heels that had been forever on the rise, the excesses of the Georgian period were ultimately reined in by domestic economics and foreign revolution. It was now no surprise that in the Regency period that followed (1795–1830) it was to be a woman's waist that was to take an upward turn. Historically the focus of a woman's body, it appeared no longer satisfied with its natural position and so for upward of

'Fashions of the Day – or Time past & Time Present – 1740 a ladies dress of bombazine / the year 1807 a ladies undress of 'bum-be-seen', from *La Belle Assemblée*. (Author's collection)

twenty years was to be located so high under a woman's breasts as to become invisible. No less than a godsend for the Regency woman, she could suddenly enjoy a freedom of dress that her grandmothers could only have dreamed of. Gone were heavy silks and brocades, the swathes of incongruous petticoats and breath-robbing corsets of previous centuries. Dresses 'à la grecque' evolved from a European pre-occupation with all things Greek and Roman and occurred as early as the 1790s, even though the Regency period in English history did not strictly start until 1811. These changes in fashion favoured the natural contours of the body, draping the female form in gauzy, diaphanous fabrics and were inspired by the French Revolution, the concept of 'Enlightenment', freedom, human rights and equality, which were associated with the ancient ideals of Greece and Rome. With such a radical development in female costume in favour of less structured garments it was obvious that some women were not about to embrace the change without some thought.

As early as 1791 the *Derby Mercury* commented:

the rage at the moment is the new imported dresses of clear lawn, beautifully wrought in feather stitch which runs from ten to fifty guineas a dress! This is not likely to prove the most economical dress in the world, as it is a matter of doubt whether, from the flimsiness of its structure it will endure the clear-starcher's operation!

Engraved for the Lady's Magazine.

PARIS DRESS *Handkerchief-shawl and Apron Straw hat with the edge turned up.*

As far as the hair is concerned, the *Mercury* tells us 'the hair is now cropped short enough to leave the ear in a state of perfect nudity'. The shape and size of bonnets continued to reduce, the latest trend in female dress being that of 'littleness – little beads, little handkerchiefs, little aprons, little caps and little hats …', possibly striking fear into the fainthearted with a report that, as bonnets were no longer as deep as previously worn, 'the eye brow is scarcely arched over, so that the poor female nose is of course left to the rigid mercy of the March winds'.

As if that weren't enough Lady Elizabeth Lambert's new hat was called from its extreme flatness a 'pancake' hat, while another woman 'of taste' pointed out her headdress resembled a fritter, so small was its shape. 'Thus for the sake of fashion …', the paper continued, 'are the ladies to carry pancakes and fritter upon their heads?'. Continuing in the same vein, another lady swore she would 'for next spring' set a new

Engraving of a Parisian day dress, *Lady's Magazine*, 1802. *(Author's collection)*

trend of wearing different coloured shoes to see if the women, like sheep would follow the ridiculous fashion unquestionably.

There is no doubt that this new trend of near nudity suited Napoleon Bonaparte. With an eye on the French economy his plans to revitalise the French textile industry included a ban on trade with England. This would aid French production of fine fabrics such as tulle and batiste and it was rumoured he even had the fireplaces of the Tuileries blocked up to keep the ladies of the court chilled and therefore encourage them to wear more of such delicate fabrics. The description of these particular 'barely there' dresses which left arms uncovered and little to the imagination was at first referred to as having an 'impure waist'. The term 'Empire line' or 'Empire silhouette' did not come into being until early in the twentieth century.

With the waist rising to the highest point it would attain in this period, fashion became svelte and streamlined for the first time since the Middle Ages and it could reasonably be assumed there would be little room for deception. Unsurprisingly, the Regency period was as counterfeit as the preceding centuries but this time it was male fashion that was to exploit a smaller waist and a well-turned calf, especially as Napoleon decreed that gentlemen wear white satin breeches for formal occasions. With men finding fashionable extremes both ridiculous and unsustainable common sense prompted the introduction of the trouser as we know it today.

It was George Bryan Brummell, more commonly known as 'Beau' (1778–1840), who epitomised the masculine ideal of the Regency period. The adoption of the frock coat, or coat, in the preceding Georgian period had with its corresponding waistcoat and britches in effect unified the male body within what we would recognise today as a three-piece suit. With the *Guardian* newspaper stating in 1713 that 'to keep to the propriety of dress the coat, waistcoat and breeches must be of the same Piece ...', these garments remained constant for almost a century, the cut and materials used in their construction the only things that rang any changes. Britches, however, left the lower part of a man's legs encased in stockings or hose which for the fashion conscience meant a well-turned calf. Such were the pressures for men both young and old to display a shapely limb that false calves were purchased. But once a falsehood becomes the norm to be without the deception is to fall short of expectations. Such anxiety accompanied one young man soon after he had secured the affections of one young lady, to disastrous effect. Once in her bedchamber he managed to secret his false calves under the pillows before the object of his desire returned to the room from her antechamber. Unfortunately, his anguish was such at the thought of having to replace them in the morning – unseen by his love – ultimately ruined all attempts at lovemaking leaving both parties quite unsatisfied.

George Bryan 'Beau' Brummell (7 June 1778–30 March 1840). He established the mode of dress for men that rejected overly ornate fashions for one of understated, fitted and tailored garments.

Brummell is arguably responsible for the introduction of the male 'trouser', a garment that if it had been adopted by the aforementioned gentleman would have saved him much embarrassment. Brummell's tailors were Schweitzer & Davidson, in Cork Street, as well as a German gentleman named Meyer, who lived in Conduit Street, London. Between

Dandies Dressing, Cruikshank, 1818. *(Library of Congress)*

them the 'trouser' which was open at the bottom of the leg and closed by buttons and loops was invented. It was, nevertheless, a change in men's clothing that was both accepted and disowned in equal measure.

In 1821 it was reported in the newspapers that gentlemen who adhered to the new stylish trousers were denied entry into certain fashionable clubs and society venues, one patroness of a venue refusing entry to gentlemen 'who not complying with the rules laid down respecting tights, present themselves in shapeless trowsers, vulgarly call'd whites'. This included the Duke of Wellington in one instance. The paper also added, 'Tis rumour'd that in consequence large orders for false calves' were made 'to grace the spindle shanks of those whom nature made by halves'.

This discrepancy over fashion was the subject of both humour and derision in political circles, providing opportunities to lampoon those in power. With talk of 'false calves' still a current topic despite being out of fashion in 1828, the reference was used to try and discredit prominent politicians, Lord Palmerston being a case in point. 'Some of Palmerston's political acquaintances …', dared report one satirist of the then Foreign Secretary, 'declare that he has a false tongue. We know that he carries about him false hair, false calves, false teeth, false eyebrows and other false articles, but a false tongue is rather too great a stretch of the power of art over nature.' Yet, in 1858 when Palmerston was 68 and England's Prime Minister he was still being accused by his opponents of not being what he seemed. Charging him with being envious of the legs of his own footmen, they put about the rumour that he still enlarged his calves with cork. This was particularly cutting as by now, the middle of the nineteenth century, stockings and shapely calves had been relegated solely to servant's attire and so did nothing to endorse Palmerston's prestige.

But it was not only trousers that Brummell had introduced to the unsuspecting male populous. From the mid-1790s, Beau Brummell's celebrity status popularised wearing clean clothing and bathing. It was much needed in an era where many people including notaries and aristocrats, such as Charles James Fox and the Duke of Norfolk (Charles Howard 1746–1815), were notoriously filthy. When the Duke was complaining one day to a gentleman that he had tried everything possible to cure his rheumatism Brummell supposedly replied, 'Pray, my Lord, did you ever try a clean shirt?'

Tall and fair with a rakish broken nose due to a fall from a horse, Brummell was the son of the private secretary of Lord North and became the benefactor of his father's will, including an inheritance of £20,000, aged just 16. After a brief time in the military, he decided to give up his captaincy, took a house in Chesterfield Street, Mayfair, avoided all extravagance such as gaming and kept only one pair of horses. Essentially what was to become known as a dandy, his love of dressing well and personal cleanliness became legend with him setting the trend for other Regency gentlemen. Being a dandy was much admired, though the term has become derogatory today, and his style turned the tide against what had up until now seen men overdressed, over made-up, effeminate, powdered and be-wigged. In short, a 'fop'. Such men in the years leading up to Brummell's introduction into society were loath to relinquish their eighteenth-century shirt, very much visible and adorned with lace, especially at the wrist which necessitated large sometimes overblown hand gestures to keep the fabric out of the way and keep it clean. A fop's whole body language had evolved to cater for the outmoded form of dress and rendered him an object of ridicule in the face of Brummel's clean-cut elegance. Men emulating the new trend now had plain starched cuffs, allowing only an inch or so of material to be visible below the edge of their coat sleeve. It was at about this time that 'shooting one's cuffs' came about as men would regularly pull down or adjust their cuffs to ensure they extended properly. It wasn't only shirts that Brummel influenced as he reined in colour and cut, introducing the monochrome palette and clean lines. It was he that laid down the first Ascot dress code by decreeing that black and white should be the basis of the male 'morning suit', while ladies should regard the occasion as 'a competition of elegance, as much so as a court ball'.

To watch Brummell dress was a privilege indeed and he opened his house most mornings for those (including the Prince Regent, later to become George IV) who wanted to watch him wash and clothe himself. Possibly his trademark innovation to the fashion of the time was the neck cloth (neckerchief) over which he was meticulous. Previously, the cloth at a man's neck was unstiffened, causing it to sit untidily in front of him. Brummel introduced starch to the fabric then went about fashioning his neck cloth until it was the epitome of elegance, a model that was imitated by all fashionable gentleman.

It was said that his valet one day descended the stairs while Brummel was dressing in his room with a large 'quantity of tumbled neck-cloths under his arm', and being asked by one of those who had come to watch Brummel dress was simply told 'Oh, these are our failures.' Such was Brummel's way of practising to make perfect. A friend, privy to these trials, tells us of the amusing way Brummel ensured the success of the accessory:

> The collar which was always fixed to his shirt, was so large that before being folded down it completely hid his head and face; and the white neck-cloth was at least a foot in height. The first maneuver made with the shirt collar was to fold it down to its proper size, which Brummell, then standing before the mirror with his chin poked up to the ceiling, by the gentle and gradual declension of his lower jaw, creased the cravat to reasonable dimensions the form of each succeeding crease being perfected.

By 1810 the folding and tying of neck-cloths had become such an art, Beau Brummell declared it took him upwards of an hour each morning to perfect his knot!

Unfortunately, Brummel fell out of favour with the Prince, his voice which was described as 'very pleasing' eventually directed one too many inappropriate remarks at his royal patron. After gambling his way to ruin, he fled to France where despite his lack of money continued to live beyond his means. Eventually becoming feeble-minded, he fell as far from his iconic self as it was possible to go. A book on his life written in 1844 by a Captain Jesse gives us a glimpse of his terrible fall from grace.

> I have deferred writing for some time, hoping to be able to inform you that I had succeeded in getting Mr Brummell into one of the public institutions, but I am sorry to say that I have failed. I have also tried to get him into a private house, but no one will undertake the charge of him in his present state. In fact, it would be totally impossible for me to describe the dreadful situation he is in. For the last two months I have been obliged to pay a person to be with him night and day, and still we cannot keep him clean. He now lies upon a straw mattress, which is changed every day. They will not keep him at the hotel, and what to do I know not. I should think that some of his old friends in England would be able to get him into some hospital where he could be taken care of for the rest of his days. I beg and entreat of you to get something done for him, for it is quite out of the question that he can remain where he is. The clergyman and physician here can bear testimony to the melancholy state of idiocy he is in.

The man who had singlehandedly ousted the fop and trailblazed the dandy to an over-indulgent and tired Georgian world died in 1840 in the madhouse of Bon Succour.

As the trouser was adopted and men's legs effectively lengthened women were also coming to terms with their new-found freedom of dress. Some were delighted with the new Empire line while others were more circumspect, seeing it as 'odd' and believing they had literally 'lost their waist'. The transparency of fabrics also caused concern as they were described in the press as being both 'too adhesive' to the body and 'too transparent and unsuited to our climate'. With

An original hand-coloured Paris fashion plate from La Mode gents' outfits, April 1834. *(Author's collection)*

PATENT·BOLSTERS: _ Le moyen d'etre en-bon point .

Mrs Fitz-Herbert

Caricature depicting Mrs Fitzherbert standing at her dressing table, about to tie a pad on her breasts to make her very buxom figure even plumper! Her stays are pushing her bust upwards to form the characteristic 'shelf', where the chin is sometimes hidden between the 'invading mounds'! *(Courtesy of the Victoria and Albert Museum)*

the extensive use of sarcenet and muslins it was also thought that the whole fashion was 'ill calculated to protect against damp, cold and fog'.

A short-lived fashion introduced itself in the spring of 1805. 'Several of our young dames of distinction …', reported the *Salisbury and Winchester Journal* of April 1805, 'now sport muslin trousers, under a white petticoat, short enough to exhibit them to full view. It is, however, a moot point at present, whether this new fashion be intended to conceal indifferent legs or to draw the gazers eye more attentively to good ones.'

With focus away from the waist it was now the turn of the breasts to be celebrated once more, and for the first time receive a purpose-made undergarment employed exclusively in the task of moulding them. Needless to say, breasts soon became the focus of the press's attention regarding their whereabouts and exposure. The *Morning Herald* published a scathing piece on the 'new' position of the breast saying:

> The bosom, which Nature planted at the bottom of a woman' chest, is pushed up by means of wadding and whalebone to a station so near her chin that in a very full subject that feature is sometimes lost between the invading mounds. The stays – or coat of mail – must be laced as tight as strength can draw the cord, Not only is the shape thrust out of its proper place but the blood is thrown forcibly into the face, neck and arms … and were it not for the fine apparel of our ladies we should be at a loss at the first glance to decide, by their redundancy and universal redness, whether they were nurses or cooks. Over this strangely manufactured figure a scanty petticoat and as scanty a gown are put. The latter resembles a bolster-slip rather than a garment.

Regency 'short stays'. For the first time a lady's undergarment began to support and shape the bosom as opposed to compressing it. *(Photograph Tessa Hallmann)*

What is evident from our understanding of the Regency bosom is that it was located as high under a woman's chin as it was possible to go. Corsets and stays in previous centuries were designed primarily to trim the waist. To be comfortable a woman had to manoeuvre her assets in such a way that when lacing took place and her figure rendered into a cone shape her breasts were not pressed downward but flattened against the bodice. As a consequence, the top half of her bosom appeared rounded and depending on how tight she laced her waist and how low the neckline of her dress, her cleavage could either be ample or modest. Even so, the result was usually a 'heaving bosom' due to vice-like lacing which compressed the ribs and so shortened breathing causing the chest to rise and fall rapidly giving every woman the appearance of a giddy girl in a constant swoon over whatever a gentleman might say.

The softer long stays and new short stays of the nineteenth century were much easier for a woman to wear with the introduction of darts to sculpt the garment. This underpinning now catered for the woman's shape effectively supporting a woman's bust yet inadvertently creating another problem. Depending on just how a lady wished to present herself, she now had the option of offering up her delights to a staggering height. The new silhouette was known later as the Great Regency Shelf.

As with every other fashion from time immemorial, opinions were voiced as to propriety and morals and the effect of short stays was no exception. A male writer observing the fashion of exposing the bosom wrote, 'A woman, proud of her beauty, may possibly be nothing but a coquet: one who makes a public display of her bosom, is something worse.' Others simply enjoyed lampooning the fashion as with this tale of two gentlemen conversing over a lady at a

Outdoor wear, 1807. *(Author's collection)*

ball. Upon seeing how she had somehow managed to hoist her bosom so high under her chin as to render her chin barely visible, they then wagered whether the lady could possibly be able 'to rest a dish of tea' upon the resulting 'rising moons' and not spill a drop!

A small book aimed at giving advice to women as to the correct way to dress and behave called *The Mirror of the Graces by A Lady of Distinction* also commented, 'Let the youthful female exhibit without shade as much of her bust as shall come within the limits of fashion, without infringing on the borders of immodesty. Let the fair of riper years appear less exposed. To sensible and tasteful women a hint is merely required.' Another book, *The Arts of beauty; or secrets of a ladies toilet: with hints to Gentlemen on the Art of Fascinating* by Madame Lola Montez, Countess of Landsfeld, also advised:

> The bosom, which nature formed with exquisite symmetry in itself, and admirable adaptation to the parts of the figure to which it is united, has been transformed into a shape, and transplanted to a place, which deprives it of its original beauty and harmony with the rest of the person. This hideous metamorphose has been effected by means of newly invented stays or corsets which, by an extraordinary construction and force of material, force the figure of the wearer into whatever form the artist pleases … In consequence we see, in eight women out of ten, the hips squeezed into a circumference little more than the waist; and the bosom shoved up to the chin, making a sort of fleshy shelf, disgusting to the beholders, and certainly most incommodious to the bearer.

Newspapers were instrumental in guiding both ladies and gentlemen towards what fashions were on the horizon, with updates every month as to what to embrace with a passion or avoid like the plague. The public, only too willing to be led, were eager to oblige. On Tuesday, 4 April 1809 the *Hull Packet*, a four-page publication that had made its debut in 1787 and sold at an expensive 7 pence, informed the ladies that their Full dress should be of white satin with long sleeves slashed at the top, a mantle of purple, edged with swansdown, gold net cap with white feathers, white shoes, gloves and fan topped off by a necklace, earrings and other ornaments 'in gold'. Her Walking Dress was also described in great detail, mentioning a tunic of silk, a cloak of the same colour, bonnet and boots, a raised spotted muslin underdress with loose sleeves bound at the arm and wrist, gold necklace and York tan gloves. Such newspapers were the fashion magazines of the day and general observations thrown in for good measure give us a glimpse of the new neo-Grecian dresses complete in their scandalous diaphanous fabrics along with comical comments. Speaking of how one particular colour did not suit everyone, the *Hull Packet* continued: 'Red cloaks are at length completely abandoned and we congratulate our lovely readers on their own emancipation from the most despotic dress colour that ever was introduced by the whimsical and arbitrary goddess of fashion. Our promenades presented us with an assemblage of pallid and ghastly spectres who appeared to be literally robed in flame.'

Green, for that spring of 1809, was not about to fare any better than its fiery cousin, as reported in the *Chester Courant* on Tuesday, 11 April 1809:

> Pea-green is a colour generally introduced in spring – for what reason we know not – except it be intended to harmonise with the verdure, with which at this season, all nature is beginning to be clothed. We entreat our fair readers not to adopt a colour so directly in opposition to good taste and in which no face of form can ever appear with advantage and effect.

On the other hand, some colours were definitely to be worn, 'lilac, purple all the variations of blue, with the still variations of grey, are open to their choice. If green must be selected let it be the deep and rich hue of Spanish fly rather than the worst and vilest of colours, pea-green.'

A fashion plate from 1824 showing a lady's travelling costume. The hem is widening and the waist is beginning to descend. *(Author's collection)*

Newspapers alone were not sufficient to satisfy the voracious appetite ladies had for fashion news and the late eighteenth century saw a blossoming of periodicals for women, some with more than a passing interest in fashion. The *Lady's Magazine*, full title the *Lady's Magazine 'or Entertaining Companion for the Fair Sex Appropriated Solely for their Use and Amusement'*, was first published in 1770. It continued well into the 1830s, its fifty-five pages concerned with improving women's minds with biographical and historical essays, instructional pieces on natural history, geography, botany, short or serialized fiction, poetry as well as reviews of new books and plays. After 1800, one hand-coloured fashion print was included and after 1815 there were two. Retailing at sixpence for the first twenty-five years, in 1805 it doubled its price to a shilling. Its highest ever price was 2 shillings and sixpence in 1828 and it proved to be a popular general interest publication marketed as a product that would suit both 'the housewife as well as the peeress'.

In 1806, John Bell, publisher of the *Morning Post* newspaper and many other books and periodicals, launched *La Belle Assemblée*, or *Bell's Court and Fashionable Magazine addressed particularly to the Ladies* with each monthly issue selling for 3 shillings sixpence for forty-eight pages. As well as providing mind-improving content, as did the *Lady's Magazine*, he offered more fashion coverage with quality illustrations and detailed advice on dress. Several columns were given over to 'General observations on Fashion & Dress' which commented on who was wearing what and how in public but being ever polite it never named names but used references such as 'a lady of rank'. A staple feature of both magazines was the observational accounts of 'The Royal Drawing Room' twice yearly in January and June. This was in honour of the king and queen's birthdays and described in meticulous detail what was being worn by the lords and ladies at court. A popular feature, this successfully appeased the voracious appetites of Regency women for the latest news, fashion and gossip.

Ackerman's *Repository of Arts, Literature, Commerce, Manufacture, Fashions and Politics* (1790–1829) was an expensive publication out of the reach of all except the upper classes. Selling at 4 shillings for 64 pages, its circulation was approximately 2,000 copies per month with 6 hand-coloured engravings, 2 of which were on fashion, and in its early days it also included small swatches of fabric from sellers who advertised with them. An engraver by trade, Ackerman was born in Germany, moving to England where in 1796 he opened a print shop which by 1809 was the largest in London. From the outset Ackerman's publication provided beautiful fashion plates with the highest quality engravings and most delicate hand colouring.

Other magazines had their place including the highly successful *Lady's Monthly Museum*, or *Polite Repository of Amusement and Instruction: being an Assemblage of what can tend to Please the Fancy, Instruct the Mind or Exalt the Character of the British Fair*, a publication with a title almost as long as its sixty-two pages! There was also *Le Beau Monde*, 1806–10. *La Miroir de la Mode* was a short-lived, expensive and large quarto-sized magazine, while the *Magazine of the Female Fashions of London and Paris*, 1799–1806, was the second magazine to be devoted entirely to fashion with distinctive prints that often featured real women, such as Emma, Lady Hamilton. The first such magazine was Nikolaus von Heideloff's *Gallery of Fashion*. Subscription-based and costing a prohibitive 3 guineas per year, the equivalent today of almost £120, this early magazine (1794–1803) had a most distinguished clientele. At that price it is not surprising there were only 450 copies printed, though one distinguished subscriber was the queen.

By 1817 the stark neoclassical outlines of Empire gowns at the turn of the century had given way to a fancier outline, with decoration added both at the top of the gown and at its hem. Fabrics were still very fine with muslin, cotton fabrics, linen and lawn favoured overall. The waist was still firmly located under the bosom but by now the outline of the skirt was becoming most definitely 'bell-shaped'. A description from the July edition of *La Belle Assemblée* of 1817 describes a typical day outfit:

Round dress of cambric, with two embroidered flounces, divided at about half a quarter of a yard, with rows of small tucks. Colerette body of fine cambric, ornamented round the bust and at the bottom of the waist to correspond with the border of the dress. Leghorn bonnet ornamented with puffings of pink satin. Lyonese shawl of grass-green with a narrow variegated border. Pink kid shoes, and Limerick gloves.

The *London's Morning Post* in 1819 mentioned how evening dresses were becoming less classical and although 'plain white transparent gauze frocks were to be worn over a white satin slip', the skirt now could be 'surrounded by rows of the most novel and tasteful trimming we have seen for a considerable time'. The article described an afternoon gown as a 'Round dress of fine plain India muslin, with triple flounces richly embroidered …', and also mentioned the latest garment to keep a lady warm in the face of all that diaphanous fabric, namely an open 'Spencer' of ethereal blue.

Originally, the Spencer jacket was worn by men in the 1790s as an extra warm layer over a tailed coat. Frequently decorated with military frogging, it is thought that Earl Spencer created the garment unawares when he stood too close to a fire and the tails of the jacket were badly singed. Cutting them off he was left with a long-sleeved tail-less jacket which was later adopted by females and became the 'look' of the Regency period and immortalised by the books and writings of the author Jane Austin. Just as a cardigan is worn today, the Spencer was a garment for both indoor and outside use, every day and special occasions. When worn with an evening gown it was usually made of silk or kerseymere (a fine woollen cloth with a fancy twill weave) and called a canezou. The Spencer became a mainstay of women's fashion during the twenty years

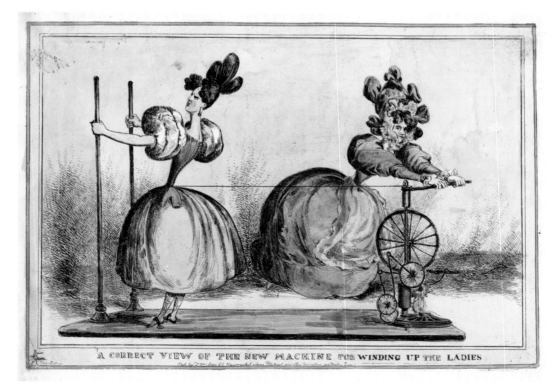

'A correct view of the new machine for winding up the Ladies.' This cartoon by William Heath is a parody of the fashion for tightly cinched waists and hugely padded sleeves of the time, *c.* 1829. *(Courtesy of Yale University)*

that the waistline remained elevated and was highly decorated in military fashion, embracing braids, buttons, quilting and cording, only becoming longer when the woman's waist itself descended once more.

As a consequence of a lady's waist returning to where nature had originally intended, fashion dictated that women again adopt the fussy full skirts and preposterous sleeves of previous centuries and once more visibly corset herself, putting an end to the freedom of mind and body she had so briefly enjoyed.

CHAPTER 8

Death by Crinoline

*'Even the prime minister has spoken out against the Crinoline in Parliament – they may as well
have spoken out against gravity or the tides!'*

Dundee, Perth & Cupar Advertiser, 1862

There was no more a contentious Victorian fashion, both for the 'fair sex' who wore it and the male population who were forced to accommodate it, than the crinoline. Even the corset with its propensity to give the wearer 'tight-laced Liver', as quoted in Dr Sir Frederick Treves's *The Influence of Clothing on Health* (Cassell, 1886), or permanent disfigurement if worn at too young an age only affected the woman who wore it invisibly beneath her clothes. The crinoline on the other hand was 'a monster'. Fathers and husbands hated them, politicians tried to

Crinolines effectively isolated women in a sea of fabric, *Punch* cartoon, 1856. *(Author's collection)*

legislate against them, Florence Nightingale decried them and employers banned them. Letters from angry readers about the 'ridiculous skirt' in the pages of top London newspapers and *Punch* magazine lampooned the fashion but to no avail.

One Dundee newspaper reported, on 15 August 1862:

> Crinoline has gone on expanding year by year till it has reached today's preposterous dimensions. Expostulation is useless. You may reason with a lady about the expense of the fashion; you can appeal to her whether she finds the dress heavy and inconvenient and see how monstrous and indelicate it looks on others; you may point out how uncomfortable it is to walk by her side, that it precludes her from almost every rapid and graceful motion, stops her from moving in confined spaces; makes her a nuisance in an omnibus or carriage and even on public streets. You may as well talk to a stone.

In its condemnation of the latest female fashion the paper had certainly echoed what every man in the country was thinking. It went on to conclude: 'Crinoline at present must be considered a necessary evil but hope it proves to be a temporary one'.

But what was so undesirable about a multitude of frothy petticoats designed simply to shape a skirt? The crinoline was in fact a cage encasing the lower body and distorting it into, at its peak, as reported in a contemporary newspaper, 'a full domed contour akin to a tea-pot cover'. Popular for just over a decade from 1860, it grew in size until it was, among other things, totally at odds with the size of doorways. Town housing was becoming smaller, though no less cluttered, and it was to prove totally unsuitable for huge skirts or, in the case of families with many daughters and female servants, no less than veritable fleets of women in full sail.

Crinoline first appeared as a linen material interwoven with horsehair used for cloth petticoats; the French *crin* and *lin*, meaning horsehair and linen respectively. Gone were the soft high-waisted shapes of the first decades of the nineteenth century, diaphanous evening gowns and

Dressing for the ball in 1857, from *Follies of the Year: a series … from Punch's Pocket Books 1844–1866* (London, Bradbury, Evans & Co., 1868). *(Author's collection)*

cotton and muslin day dresses which fell in a body-skimming column from just beneath the bosom. These were nudged aside by the reintroduction of the waist, albeit higher and wider. At last in 1856 the metal cage crinoline was introduced by the American W. S. Thompson. This lightweight support enabled ladies to wear just one petticoat to soften the cage ridges, and also saw the introduction of another new item of clothing, namely women's drawers. Up until now there had been no need for such an undergarment as the weight of petticoats prevented

An antique print showing ladies' daywear, *c.* 1850s. *(Author's collection)*

skirts blowing about in the wind. These layers had steadily grown in number until by 1840 no less than six petticoats were normally worn and with no indication that such padding was likely to reduce, organ, flat and cartridge pleats had added even more volume, effectively bringing a woman to a standstill within her own clothes. Yet, now sporting no more than a lightly covered cage, a woman suddenly found herself having to grapple with that enemy of the crinoline, blustery weather and so to save her innocent blushes an appropriate undergarment was quickly found.

What made the fashion for the crinoline so popular was the fact it was universal, adopted by every woman in the Western world. In 1861 the *Dundee Courier* reported that even servants wore the skirt, and commented on its abject impracticality: 'Unlike former times of hoops and vardingales the fashion has even descended to servants, so that where the dining room is small table maids have been known to give warning because they could not clear the space between the table and the fire and the newspapers are continually announcing "Accident from crinoline or woman burned to death". The only difference seemed to be the quality of the crinoline across the social orders, with ugly ridges of steel bands visible through thin fabrics for wearers among the working class. Yet, young, old, fat and thin wore the hoop, and with such universal female appeal Sheffield, at the height of the crinoline's popularity, was producing enough steel to equip women with ½ million hoops in one week.

In an effort to curtail its use it was once suggested the hoop should only be available for 'mature' women, matrons whose movements were less frivolous and so less of a problem for anyone within 6ft of them. Surprisingly, men had limited influence over their womenfolk's adoration for the garment with warnings as to its dangers largely ignored by their wives and daughters. If they had taken more notice perhaps there would have been less of an outcry for the overblown and incredulous fashion, and fewer sorry tales of the disproportionate deaths and accidents to both male and female alike in the national and international press.

There is no doubt that accidents as a direct result of wearing a crinoline were more frequent than with any other garment in history. In addition, it was the only fashion where not only the wearer but also anyone within a short distance of them was at risk of disaster. Fire was the most common hazard with grisly accounts frequently appearing in the press. The death of Mary Anne Winterbotham, aged 22, was described in the *Shoreditch Observer* in 1861. She had picked up a shovel-full of burning coals to light the drawing room fire and placed it on the ground while she stooped to get wood from a cupboard. Her dress must have swept over the coals and as she was wearing a cane crinoline the garment rapidly caught fire. The jury returned a verdict of accidental death but expressed horror and disgust that someone whose household duties brought them in contact with hearth fires still chose to wear the inflated fashion.

Yet accidents could happen even when the lady in question was not performing a hazardous domestic task. In 1862 17-year-old Mary Anne Lane of Bedford found herself aflame when she stooped, 'leant', forward to dress her hair in a looking glass placed on the dining table. In doing so her crinoline billowed out behind her towards the lit fire in the grate, where the back of her dress was instantly engulfed. Despite her family at considerable risk to themselves tearing away nearly all of her clothes and wrapping her in a large quilt, she died from her injuries 'and subsequent shock of having been badly burned about the legs', as reported in the *Worcestershire Chronicle* on 14 May 1862. A year later it was reported that 16-year-old servant Maria Agnes Devonshire had died while wearing a crinoline. As part of her duties she washed the children's faces in the mornings and as she stooped down her crinoline was forced between the bars of the fire grate. She instantly caught fire and ran in terror into the garden. Her master, hearing her screams, rushed into the garden but before he could extinguish the flames Maria had received fatal injuries.

Men complained bitterly in heartfelt letters to editors beseeching women to realise the dangers of their dress. One man raised his concerns in the *Morning Post* in 1861, signing himself simply 'a father':

The risks incurred every hour of every day by the wearer of a crinoline dress cannot be denied. Ingenuity is at a loss to devise a costume more dangerous from fire than this balloon-like apparatus attached to the female form. Our low open fire-places, candles, Lucifer matches, the simple act of sealing a letter, is pregnant with danger. Can any condemnatory of this detestable costume be too strong?

In 1864 a Dr Lancaster reported there had been 2,500 deaths in London alone from fire on account of the monstrous skirt. Reactions from the public were becoming noticeably weary, at

July 7 1937   PUNCH *or The London Charivari*   27

THE CRINOLINE

Chair Proprietor. " Would you please to pay for the chairs, Mum?"
Lady. " How much?"
Chair Proprietor.—Well, Mum—how many might you be a sittin' on?"

John Leech, July 9th, 1859.

A look back at ladies' fashion, *Punch* magazine, 1937. The original was by John Leech, 1859. *(Author's collection)*

times bordering on the impatient, 'At all events if crinoline must be the fashion then every lady should wear a fire screen or at least be attended by a maid with an extinguisher' was one terse suggestion. As early as 1859 *Punch* magazine reported that 'Unless dresses are made fire-proof, no one, while the present stuck-out fashion lasts, can wear them safely. As a deterrent from wide petticoats we should pass an Act of Parliament to regulate their sale, and should permit none to be worn without being marked "DANGEROUS!"'

Punch also joked that were there ever a crinoline insurance company established it could not possibly withstand the constant claims, fire escapes should be provided in all drawing rooms and air tubes within the petticoat might all be filled with water (and a means to eject it) thus making every lady her own fire engine. Needless to say, none of these schemes came to fruition.

In June 1863 even something as mundane as climbing stairs posed a serious threat. Despite the introduction of strings, hinges and pulley systems attached to the underside of the skirt to help with raising the front of the hoop, the wife of a merchant still caught her foot in her crinoline and fell with such violence she fractured her skull. Even the genteel and sedate pursuit of archery became a hazard when in Hertfordshire the wife of a clergyman suddenly sat down on the grass snapping one of the steel hoops which supported her dress. The sharp end penetrated a tender part of her body and inflicted a severe internal wound. Another lady from Bath, while standing talking with friends, was unaware her dress was extending across a footpath and was accidentally dragged along the ground when a delivery cart drove past and its step hooked into her crinoline. Both of the woman's legs were broken.

With women's common sense refusing to prevail, men at least united against the hoop in satire and wit. 'Men having tolerated crinolines long enough and patiently, are now claiming they have a right to comment on the situation ...', rallied one newspaper. Comment they did, gentlemen taking every opportunity to complain and commiserate with each other about how hard it had become for a man to live harmoniously with the women in his life while they were blindly in thrall to the ridiculous fashion, as revealed in this quote from the *Era*, Sunday, 24 May 1864:

> Ladies cannot accuse us of intruding in any way upon the mysteries of the Female toilette in fact most men devoutly wish that the crinoline was indeed a mystery on the contrary it invades us on all levels in all places; at home and abroad, in the domestic circle, at the ball, opera, lecture room and at church in the streets on the omnibus is not every man made perfectly aware (chiefly through contact with his shins) that women as well as ships are 'iron-clad'.

But it was not just a man's dignity that was lost on contact with crinoline. Men were in danger of being killed by their wives' and daughters' skirts. In one instance when a man tried to pass a woman in a busy street, his foot caught in her crinoline and he fell into the gutter where a passing brewer's dray ran over him, crushing his legs, Although taken to hospital, he died four days later, but during his time there, instead of blaming the driver of the vehicle in his report to the police, he wholeheartedly blamed the woman wearing the crinoline. In total agreement the lord mayor, hearing of this terrible accident, urged the police to exonerate the driver of the dray and prosecute the woman and her crinoline. The police never managed to trace the woman in question.

Accidents outside the home also proved fatal, proving there was no room for such a skirt in the workplace. In 1860, the textile firm Courtauld's instructed their workers 'to leave Hoop and Crinoline at Home', but for one young woman, a 17-year-old factory worker employed, ironically, in a crinoline factory in Sheffield, there was no such advice. The *Essex Standard* of 1860 reported:

Sarah Ann Murfin age 17 – ascended a ladder to the upper floor to ask for a companion. The ladder was three feet from wall and between it and the wall is revolving shaft used drive machinery. Her skirt (much extended by crinoline) entangled in this machinery and she screamed for assistance but before shaft could be stopped. It whirled her round a great number of times her head and other parts of her body being dashed against the wall and the joists of the floor above & the ladder.

The poor girl was dead when they released her from the machinery, her skull dreadfully fractured, leg nearly torn off and body shockingly injured.

Even the invention of the collapsible crinoline did not prevent minor accidents or lessen fears in doctors. 'The effects of wearing this weight of hoops and petticoats round the waist are dreadful …', wrote one doctor in a letter to the *London Standard* in 1863, 'Hernia has increased to a frightful extent and varicose veins and permanent and most serious injuries to portions of the abdominal area such as the public have no idea!' He also added that were he a young man he would now hesitate to marry any girl, unless he could be convinced she was in a proper state of health, '… least I should find myself tied to a thing of hoops and petticoats whom I ought to have taken to the nearest hospital instead of to church!'.

Yet even in the house of God crinoline was unwelcome, denounced for taking up more space than churches could afford. One vicar strongly reminded his congregation that churches were not designed for the present exaggerated proportions of ladies and poured shame on those who by wearing the hoop prohibited the devout in his flock from finding a seat in order to hear the Gospel. In some cases reasons were more personal as one clergyman actually petitioned his council by letter asking for a by-law to be introduced which would directly help his position; either that or increase his stipend to accommodate the influence of the crinoline. He explained

'A Splendid Spread' by George Cruikshank, *The Comic Almanack*, 1850. Such was the impracticality of the crinoline that at parties ladies had to be fed by their companions as it was impossible for them to access the buffet tables themselves. *(Author's collection)*

that he only earned £60 per year and as 'crinolines make a dress very expensive and puffs up the female mind with unnecessary vanity ...' his daughter was putting him to enormous expense by the current inflated style of dress. Worse than that, his friend too 'had eight daughters wearing hoops!'.

For some it apparently proved too much and a Mr William Huntingdon, corn and flour merchant of Liverpool, was charged with 'cutting away a ladies crinoline' at the town assizes. It appears he had already assaulted two young ladies in Prince's Park, Liverpool previously and cut off the crinoline of the elder one, exclaiming 'These hoops, these hoops, I cannot tolerate them', or words to that effect. He was actually acquitted to loud cheers, the support mostly coming from like-minded men who looked upon him as their champion.

But as much as people took against the fashion, with an Anti-Crinoline League existing for a while, there were those that wholeheartedly embraced the trend. In a letter to the editor of the *Morning Post* in 1861, one woman eloquently pointed out that as the crinoline was so popular and universal not to wear one would be 'quaint to absurdity'. She also pointed out that the risk to crinoline from fire could be easily remedied without detracting from the grace or comfort of the fashion simply by changing the fabric used to make them from flimsy gauzes to wool and silk.

The fabrics produced in the present day are so many, so elegant and varied that there is no kind of difficulty in selecting dresses from 10 shillings to 20 guineas, perfectly un-inflammable and which if held close contact with fire would but slowly smoulder. My own and daughter's dresses have during this winter repeatedly touched the fireplace so as to receive the impression of the grate and if they had been of lighter material I shudder to realise where we should now certainly be ...

Rather than relinquish a dangerous and unnecessary fashion, she, while not wishing her daughters to burn, was obviously more than happy for them to 'smoulder'!

Other positive effects accredited to the wearing of crinolines were revealed in 1858 when a girl named Martha Shepherd, attempting to commit suicide, leaped from the top of the balustrade of the bridge over the Serpentine in Hyde Park. She clearly had not thought things through as while falling her crinoline expanded to its full dimensions and 'she came upon the water like a balloon floating there for several minutes', as reported in the *Ipswich Journal*. A nearby constable was able to throw her a lifeline and as she began to sink he was able to pull her safely to the shore. Similarly, in 1864 a nursemaid on losing her way on the cliffs in Newquay, Cornwall inadvertently walked too close to the edge, slipped and tumbled toward the beach below, a fall of approximately 100ft. Following the laws of aerodynamics, her crinoline expanded with air and so broke her fall to such a degree that she landed without a scratch or bruise. Such occurrences may be in the extreme but on a more mundane note one young lady using her crinoline as a form of defensive armour was at least able successfully to save herself from a savage attack by an angry dog.

However much those in favour of the crinoline lobbied, there is no denying that in one area the crinoline caused a significant rise in crime. As the skirt increased in size so did the practice of shoplifting until both reached epidemic proportions. Ingeniously fitted out with pockets and hooks, it seemed there was no end to the size and weight of objects that could be successfully hidden under a crinoline. Female shoplifters found crinoline a ready and convenient hiding place for silk, fancy lace articles and even parasols!

Margaret Toole, a well-dressed woman of about 25, was charged, according to a newspaper report in 1862, with robbery at a draper's shop. After walking about the shop looking at several articles, 'her peculiar manner' aroused the assistant's suspicions and moments later she noticed some fringing hanging down from under the woman's skirt. On calling for help, a policeman

Comical cartoon by John Leech, 1883. *(Author's collection)*

apprehended the woman not far from the shop and escorted her to the police station where it was found the woman had nine black silk mantles and two coloured silk dresses beneath her crinoline, all amounting to over £7. Needless to say, she was remanded.

Women crinoline thieves, however, were undeterred. Eliza Dreser, arrested at Hull police station, had become even bolder. Often remanded for stealing copious amounts of bed linen beneath her skirts, she lately was discovered to be hiding a set of steel fire-irons suspended from her waist. She protested they were her own but the police could find no reason why she should wish to transport such items in such a way and so she was charged.

From shoplifting it is only a short step to smuggling and a lady travelling on board a ship from Holland was suspected of such due to her strange gait while walking. Elizabeth Barbara Lorinz (a native of Holland) denied all charges, declaring she walked strangely due to pregnancy. On being searched, she was found to have no less than 5 pounds of cigars, 9 pounds of tobacco, a quantity of tea and a bottle of gin, all concealed beneath her crinoline. It was a similar case with Ellen Carey, whose arrest was featured in the *Chester Chronicle* of 1858. Described as 'a neatly dressed female', she was accused of smuggling 22 pounds of cigars within three large petticoats. As a passenger aboard the General Steam Navigation's ship *Moselle*, it was only once the ship had entered St Katherine's Dock and she was preparing to alight that she inadvertently alerted the

Tide Surveyor, Mr Gardiner, with her 'imense rotundity of dress'. When challenged, she explained that her 'blown' appearance was due to the crinoline, which every woman in the land wore and which she considered very becoming, whatever the gentleman thought on the subject. On being stripped of her skirts by a female searcher, the cigars were removed from her person and she was once more brought before her accusers, her size 'greatly diminished'. Her smuggling had cost her a £100 fine and six months' imprisonment.

Such instances simply fuelled men's and some women's abject dislike of the garment and put them under even more pressure to cope with consequences totally out of their control. 'My wife and daughters cannot go on a shopping trip or enter a shop without the finger of suspicion pointed at them' was the concern of one family man, followed by 'my wife is looked upon as a potential thief every time she leaves the house!' from another.

If women were aware of their menfolk's dislike of their dress, they were doggedly determined to ignore it, be it at home or abroad. In 1857 the *Liverpool Daily Post* reported on a ball held at the Tuilleries in Paris and alluded to how one gentleman's flattery was a cover for caustic sarcasm.

> At one point a certain lady was watching with anxiety a gentleman's approach across the ball room, her emotion becoming visible as he drew near, causing her in nervousness to spread out her already exorbitant skirt (which with the aid of boufants, flowers, flounces, and crinoline) filled the whole of the bench, burying beneath its ample folds two or three of her lesser dressed neighbours on either side.

As small talk gave way to the lady's inquiry as to what her suitor thought of her dress that evening she received this reply, 'Madam … I cannot but admire it for it recalls to mind the dearest souvenir of my soul'. 'Indeed,' exclaimed the lady her face brightening, '… and how so?' 'Why it reminded me the moment I entered the room, both in its extent and shape, of my tent in the Crimea!'

It was not only men who thought the battlefield no place for a crinoline. Florence Nightingale in 1863 warned her nurses against the use of crinoline on the grounds that if a modest woman knew the spectacle which she presented to her patients when bending over a fire, with expanded dress, she would forever renounce the obnoxious vestment. 'We don't want to go back to the high waists and scanty dresses of our grandmothers, but surely there is a happy medium?'

English steel produced the best wire for the crinoline cages. After being softened in a furnace it was scoured in acid to remove its oxidised surfce, then coated with rye and flour then specially dried. The steel, initially in thick, short rods, was then lengthened to no less than 2,000yd in order to reduce its width to ¾in, then hardened and tempered before being braided in yarn and sent to the warehouse for use in skirts. No less than 60,000yd of flattened steel wire were produced daily via this process. Ultimately made into coiled hoops, these were suspended by tapes in the form of a skirt, descending in increasing diameters from a band worn around a woman's waist.

'A Woman in a Corset is a Lie, a Falsehood, a Fiction, but for Us, this Fiction is Better than the Reality' – Eugene Chapus

It is accurate to say that the crinoline was a revolution in women's fashion, and the far-reaching consequences of which rivalled that of even the Crimean War. However, the tortuous corset, pristine, unseen and in many cases deadly, in contrast compressed the female into a fashionable 17 to 22in waist at the cost of health, beauty and ultimately of life itself.

It was no wonder that Victorian ladies 'swooned' so frequently. Prolonged corset wearing meant the internal organs were unable to grow in their natural position and there were fears that a woman's lungs could not function properly and that her liver could be almost cut in half.

The historical horror stories are appalling. One 23-year-old Parisian woman at a ball in 1859 proved to be the envy of all with her 13in waist; two days later she was found dead. An autopsy showed that her liver had been punctured by three ribs. A chambermaid who said she had extreme stomach pains was also found dead soon after; her stomach was nearly severed in half 'leaving a canal only as narrow as a raven's feather'. Medical men constantly argued against the corset and if a woman died in mysterious circumstances and was slender figured, a doctor would look for 'tight-lace liver', a malformation of the organ that signified to him the lady in question had been guilty of tight-lacing. It was also usual that doctors if suspecting 'tight-lacing' kept the fact to themselves to avoid publicity and scandal.

To be fashionable women have always made their waists smaller than they should be. It was only really in the nineteenth century that we can see the damage this did by reports appearing in newspapers warning the universal

'Arabella Maria: "Only to think, Julia dear, that our Mothers wore such ridiculous fashions as these!" Both: "Ha! ha! ha! ha!"', *Harper's Weekly*, 11 July 1857.

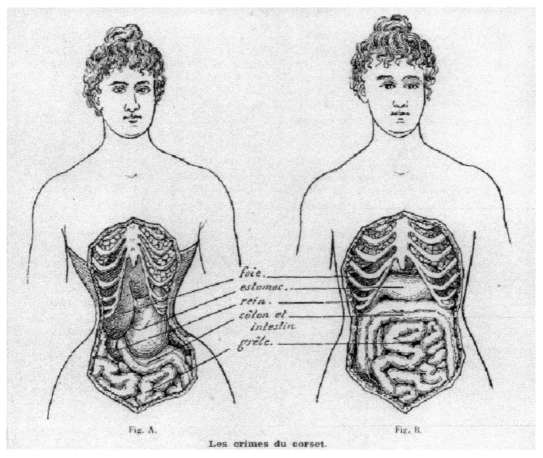

A crime of fashion. *(Wellcome Images)*

female about exactly what she was doing to herself in the name of vanity. Women had always fainted from being 'over laced' and it was a wise woman who did not conform to a hand-span waist. With improved literacy and newspaper circulation reports of extreme cases could be held up as warnings to those who would listen.

As early as 1829 reports appeared in newspapers concerned with the effects of the compression of the waist in females by the use of corsets. Pictures were also provided. It was hoped that a glance at the graphic details would bring about the change that words alone could not. A Devon newspaper published the following:

A Victorian corset, 1899. *(Library of Congress)*

Those who have long so closely laced become at last unable to hold themselves erect or move with comfort without them. The muscles of the back are weakened and crippled and cannot maintain themselves in a natural position for any length of time – the spine too no longer accustomed to bear the destined weight of the body bends and sinks down. Where tight lacing is practiced young women from 15 to 20 years of age are found so dependent upon their corsets that they faint whenever they lay them aside and therefore are obliged to have themselves re-laced before going to sleep. Or as soon as the Thorax and abdomen are relaxed by being deprived of the support the blood rushing downwards in consequence of the diminished resistance to its motion empties the vessels of the head and thus occasions fainting …

It was quite astonishing just how many diseases were attributed to tight lacing: head-aches, giddiness, fainting, pain in the eyes, pain and ringing in the ears and bleeding at the nose. In the thorax, despite the displacement of the bones and the injury done to the breast, tight lacing also produced shortness of breath, spitting of blood, consumption, derangement of the circulation, palpitation of the heart and water in the chest. In the abdomen it caused loss of appetite, squeamishness, vomiting of blood, depraved digestion, flatulence, diarrhacolic pains, dropsy and rupture. This could be followed by melancholy, hysteria and many diseases peculiar to the female constitution. It also produced what no self-respecting Victorian woman wanted – a red nose!

In 1871 the *Metropolitan* magazine ran a scathing headline which read, 'The size of the waist is more important than the size of the brain', but it appeared to have little effect. In 1881 a post-mortem on a woman named Amelia Jury, aged 43, presented a stomach constricted to an eighth of its natural size with a liver flattened and driven down deep into the pelvis. An autopsy carried out on a woman in 1895, who had mysteriously died in a dentist's chair while having a tooth extracted, showed her liver to be divided into two nearly equal parts united only by a thin channel due to tight lacing.

On a slightly lighter note, one gentleman, expressing his concerns in newsprint (complete with a diagram), wished to to make clear to ladies that their efforts to be small-waisted were not in their control at all and that female attractiveness depended entirely upon a system he himself had concocted using nothing other than algebra.

A beautiful young lady died the other evening of an inflammation of the internal region caused it is believed by the tight lacing of her corset. Let this be a warning to all fair creatures who are now tightening their corsets till their cheeks get flushed and their eyes lose all their softness and affection.

Tight lacing injures the facial beauty of a female more than they imagine. It is a mistake to imagine that a narrow female waist is so attractive in the eyes of a man. We assure our female readers that it is no such thing. We speak from feeling sentiment and natural impulse.

The slender waist is no essential element of beauty – it is part of a much wider attraction. It is necessary only to be in proportion to the rest of the female form, the whole beautiful region, the soft white neck, the pouting lips the rosy cheeks, the melting eyes and glorious angelic forehead. Milliners and corset makers who presume to set the fashions do not understand the mathematical elements of beauty that enter into the composition of graceful female forms. Among philosophers the whole theory of perfect beauty is explained in the following interesting algebraic problem … if we assume …

X	Represent the female bust
Y	Its diameter
=	Its proportions
Lm	A narrow waist
Ab	The rest of the angle

The x, y, = added to ab will be equal to the most beautiful woman that graces any salon or square – while a narrow waist only leads to death and melancholy. We trust therefore that every young and beautiful lady will study this problem and come to the inevitable conclusion that a narrow waist is not an element of beauty and grace but a principle that leads to unhappiness, pain and consumption, and finally death.

An endearing sentiment to all intents and purposes, if not a little self-serving and somewhat sexist to the modern ear?

CHAPTER 9

Bustles

'The customs officers at Queenstown on Monday arrested a passenger from New York because she had a revolver and 20 ball cartridges concealed in her bustle.'
Sunderland Daily Echo and Shipping Gazette, 1888

If Florence Nightingale called for moderation in a woman's dress it was only to fall on deaf ears. Encased in their corsets and unwilling to forego the yards of beautiful fabrics that once covered their hoops and which they had fought so hard to retain, women, with stubborn gentility, simply flattened the front of their skirts, and gathered everything up at the back into one enormous lump resulting in the equally ridiculous fashion, namely the bustle. As if that were not enough, as the century drew to a close corsetting managed to winch the female form into ever more sinuous shapes until by Edwardian times the infamous 'S' bend corset bordered not so much on the 'feminine' as the fatal.

From 1870 to the beginning of the First World War the female form underwent no less than four distinct – and equally uncomfortable – shape changes. As the crinoline quickly fell out of favour, after 1869 the female silhouette morphed from a wide shape to an upstanding one. At first tapes and ribbons were used within the skirts to achieve the new flat-fronted look by tieing and looping swathes of fabric up behind them. However, once the fashion was established women began to add more and more fabric over what was known as a 'shape improver', better known as a 'bustle' or a Grecian bend.

The first or early bustle era lasted for just under a decade from 1869 to 1876 and was a much 'softer' affair (literally) than when the fashion re-appeared with a vengeance some years later between 1883 and 1889. In this, the bustle's first incarnation, a gently rounded derrière was created by the strategic placement of small 'cages', cushions or pads, stuffed with horsehair, down or even straw. Just as with the crinoline, bustles were often

The latest French fashion, *The Ladies' Treasury*.

A horsehair bustle, 1868.

A Jupon or Tournure, 1887.

ridiculed in the press but unlike the former which was hazardous for life and limb to all who came in contact with it, the bustle was only uncomfortable for the woman who wore it.

In the *Stamford Mercury*, dated Friday, 1 May 1874, an advertisement for Thomson's novelties offered, at reasonable prices, the Corymbus, a new bustle patented and made from Chinese plaited straw. It made no bones about the fact it definitely contained 'no steel', a feature also of the Rouleau and the 'Grasshopper' Tournure (a device used by women to expand the skirt of a dress below the waist) and which would produce the very latest outline. It seems a strange phenomenon today that we were ever not in control of our own outlines and had to look elsewhere to see what we would be looking like in the near future.

Between 1877 and 1882 a far more slender silhouette became the norm, with the early bustles diminishing to leave slim hips and only a shaped petticoat to support a new trained skirt. Ruching and pleated frills emphasised the fullness of the back of the skirt but often the dress itself was so narrow a woman had to limit her stride to almost nothing. What was also evident was that to carry off such a slender style a woman had to be very slim indeed, a feat often achieved by wearing a very tight corset.

As a backlash to all this drapery a push towards simpler styles of dress was making itself known. The 1870s saw the rise of the Aesthetic Movement, which under the influences of poets, painters and actors called for beauty and grace in all things, not just dress. Its members abhorred ugliness in what they saw as products of the Industrial Revolution, rallying against harsh aniline dyes responsible for gaudy colours and called for, among other things, a stop to the use of the sewing machine which they held responsible for all the frills and flounces that masked a woman's true attractiveness. Influenced by the Pre-Raphaelite paintings of Dante Gabriel Rossetti and Edward Burne Jones, the movement held up medieval women, free of corsetry and in ethereal surroundings, as a perfect example of natural freedom. It was an ethos based primarily on aesthetics. The Rational Dress Society was formed in 1881 and was a second call to arms for those who thought it prudent, no essential that the beleaguered female was rescued from the imprisonment of her clothing and the damage it was inflicting on her health.

Advocates of practical fashions, it was Viscountess Harberton and a Mrs King who drew the nation's attention to how corsetry restricted free movement and was, if taken to extremes, fatal. On 26 March 1886 the Viscountess presided over a very well-attended lecture at Westminster

An original hand-coloured lady's fashion plate from *Der Bazar* magazine, 1885. *(Author's collection)*

The second bustle era gave ladies a curious silhouette which made the wearer's 'derrière' resemble the rear end of a horse.
Ladies Journal. (Author's collection)

Town Hall and spoke on the absurdities of feminine attire, how it was modelled upon a distorted ideal and dwelt upon the physical consequences of tight dresses. Expressing her concerns, she suggested that it was 'habit not usefulness or grace' that controlled the fashion and it was for that reason the society wished to arouse in the female mind more 'sensible aspirations'. She also explained that in her opinion tight dresses gave women high temperatures and as they also prevented exercise they were the reason so many English ladies of middle age were 'so deplorably stout'. She argued against 'the monstrosities' forced upon women by dressmakers and those in the 'trade' and was adamant that there should be reform, from 'boots to bonnets', and convinced that once the Society had enough members then opposition to women being free and safe in their clothes would melt away.

One suggestion of the Rational Dress Society was to embrace a divided skirt, but it was not universally accepted as women reasoned, quite rightly, that a divided skirt, made with enough material to make it resemble a full skirt was counter-productive, just as heavy and therefore pointless. Possibly the greatest recommendation of the Rational Dress Society was that a woman's dress should weigh no more than 1½ to 3 pounds and that her underwear should weigh no more than 7. To the modern woman who wears silk or synthetic lingerie as opposed to bulky cotton, wool or flannel this is still a great deal of clothing, but that figure was actually half of what was worn by most women in 1850 when ladies were restricted by up to 14 pounds of layered undergarments.

Among those who subscribed to the principles of the Aesthetic Movement and the Rational Dress Society was none other than the famous writer Oscar Wilde, who was more than happy to have his feelings known in an essay which appeared in the *Pall Mall Gazette* on 14 October 1884:

> all the most ungainly and uncomfortable articles of dress that fashion has ever in her folly prescribed, not the tight corset merely, but the farthingale, the vertugadin, the hoop, the crinoline, and that modern monstrosity the so-called dress improver also, all of them have owed their origin to the same error – the error of not seeing that it is from the shoulders, and from the shoulders only, that all garments should be hung.

These attempts to change women's dress had their devotees but in 1883 bustles came back with a vengeance, perhaps because some ladies thought 'women were disgusting creatures without one'. However, it was more likely to have been because Charles Frederick Worth, the designer who dominated Parisian fashion in the latter half of the nineteenth century, re-introduced the phenomena, and though skirts remained slim in front and at the sides, the back ballooned out like never before. Suddenly women were jutting out behind larger than ever and with a silhouette that made them look like they had inherited the hind legs of a horse! To remedy the difficulty in sitting, a spring-loaded bustle called a 'phantom' appeared in 1884, promising ultimate comfort as its steel wires were attached to a pivot that folded in on themselves when sat on and which sprang back when the wearer rose. Less useful was a similar novelty bustle made to commemorate Queen Victoria's Golden Jubilee celebrations, which was fitted with a musical box that played 'God Save the Queen' each time the wearer sat down.

Not about to let an opportunity pass, by 1886 companies were adding to these phenomena with the concept of a 'handbag bustle', first advertised in the *Manchester Evening News*. To all intents and purposes, said the manufacturers, its outward appearance was one of an ordinary bustle but inside there was 'a large compartment in which a lady can carry articles such as brushes, cosmetics, tooth preparations and night raiments she may require when on a short visit, or temporary absence from home'. The idea of a lady going about with her luggage in her bustle was possibly as startling to her as it is to us, but it was a great selling point and would save a woman from the problem of a lack of pockets which men did not suffer from.

The idea that bustles could double as capacious receptacles for storing items was exploited for both good and the clandestine. In 1886 a woman sorting rags at St Mary Cray Paper Mill found French coins and notes to the value of £40 in a lady's bustle, while there were reports that love letters, a gun and smuggled ammunition had been found in others. The police, out on a mission to apprehend a gang of notorious poachers, were nothing if not surprised when waiting for the men to return home with their ill-gotten gains the villains actually met the constables empty-handed. What did surprise them was that not long afterwards three women appeared to have followed them with a 'suspicious display of bustle'. On investigation, this turned out to be due to the presence of twenty-seven rabbits and two long lengths or rabbit netting. The police later commented that the inventors of a garment capable of covering such a multitude of sins had a great deal to answer for.

Alternatively, a bustle could be a cause of surprise for the unsuspecting wearer as it was for two American sisters, Misses Mamie and Della More from Pocomoke in Maryland.

After walking on their farm the women rested on a log and became engaged in conversation long enough for one sister to become aware of a heavy weight which seemed to drag her dress down behind. Asking the other to see what the matter was, the latter, after some investigation and to the horror of both women, discovered a large copper-head snake had coiled up in her bustle. Despite the snake measuring 5ft long and being as thick as a man's wrist, the ladies dealt with the intruder and continued unfazed about their business.

A similar occurrence happened to a woman in England, who after having ordered a bustle to be made for her, found it on completion to be a little too big to be fashionable and so had tucked it away in her attic until such time as it would again come into vogue. Luckily for her, it did but when she retrieved it she found it was now home to a family of house mice whom she did not have the heart to evict. Subsequently, she wore it, mice and all, the only alteration she made being a hole in the side of her bustle and her skirts so she could feed the small creatures at her dinner table which equally amused and terrified her guests.

On Saturday, 29 September 1888 an article appeared in the *Aberdeen Evening Express* detailing the strange incident of an exploding bustle. The incident happened in America in the Congregational Church of San Fransisco during a reading given by none other than novelist Charles Dickens. It appeared that a lady with a 'dignified gait' was accompanied by her husband, a military man, into the building whereupon they both found their seats. The lady gave a graceful swing to her skirt in order to sit down gracefully but at that moment a muffled but loud noise came from beneath her dress and the lady 'was observed to collapse with a lurch'. She turned deathly pale and got up looking intensely embarrassed and confused. At this point Mr Dickens stopped reading and looked up to see what was the origin of the small explosion, but finding nothing serious had happened returned to his oration. By now smiles and titters had begun to circulate the room by those who had a good idea what had happened. Unfortunately, her husband was not of a sympathetic nature and grasped his wife's arm roughly and told her not to act so foolishly. But the explosion of an inflatable bustle is no small matter to a lady and covering herself as

Punch's designs 'After Nature', snail bustle, 1870s.

much as she could with her shawl to hide her blushes she did eventually agree to stay for the evening but felt very uncomfortable doing so. Later the lady brought a law-suit against the dressmaker who made her bustle, accusing her of negligence. The dressmaker defended herself by saying that she had indeed made the bustle for her customer, several bustles in fact, in the hope that at least one would fit her as she seemed to have changed size everytime she saw her. One was deemed suitable but it was written into the contract between the dressmaker and the purchaser that the latter would not sit down suddenly and would adhere to these instructions religiously. This had obviously not been the case as the rubber bustle had indeed burst causing injury and distress to the wearer. The judge giving his decision on the merits of the case responded with the following.

'This is a most peculiar case. I have read of bustles being made of horsehair, muslin, newspapers, pillows, bird cages and even quilts. I have heard of alarm clocks striking the hour within the folds of a ladies dress. Smuggled cigars, jewelry and brandy have also been brought to light but I have never before heard of an airtight bustle exploding in church and then being made the subject of a civil suit. Not being married yet, the situation is somewhat perlexing to me, but still looking at the case from a legal standpoint, I think we can adjust matters satisfactorily. Were a non-explosive bustle used, this suit might never have been brought.' His honour then deducted a negligable sum from the bill of the dressmaker as the defendant set up a claim for damages for the explosion trouble. He then rendered judgement in favour of the plaintiff.

Undeterred by potential disasters, one woman vehemently defended her right to wear what she wanted and wrote to the *Royal Cornwall Gazette* in September 1888 to justify herself.

I wear a bustle and believe in it. I wear a large bustle and I am proud of it. I wear a steel ribbed, brass riveted, burglar and fire proof bustle, and it is a joy beyond compare. I have tried all varieties of bustle – the large and small, the round, a flat, the soft and the substantial. My experience makes me friendly to the large bustles, and the stronger they are the better I like them. The only bustle I detest is the four-cylindered affair filled with spiral wires that look like a quadruplex fire hose. The cylinders are worn vertically and if you are not careful in sitting down when you have one of these fixings on you are likely to be catapulted into the empyrean. It requires a woman of great and everlasting presence of mind to sit down properly in the 4 cylindered bustle.

I have heard time and again that men wonder how women manage to sit down wearing a bustle. The secret is that when a bustle decked women sits down she does so carefully and does so sideways. There is a pretty little trick in it. She pretends she is going to sit on the right side of the chair and makes her first movement in that direction; but just as she reaches the chair she moves gracefully to the other side, the bustle rolls to the right completely out of the way of the sitter and the problem is solved.

By the late 1880s the hard armour-like bustle was in decline, replaced by softer shape improvers which nevertheless had their downsides. On Monday, 16 January 1888 the *Dundee Courier* strongly suggested that 'Ladies Beware!'. It went on to explain how a young lady who had attended the Marlborough Races wore with pride a new and improved 'dress improver' stuffed with bran and straw. While witnessing the races she was unaware that a hungry nag stationed behind her had smelled the stuffing and thinking it for him unceremoniously tore the dress to pieces, leaving the woman in complete disarray in his endeavours to eat its contents.

YACHTING AND BOATING GOWNS. (MESSRS. SHOOLBRED AND CO. *See page* 92.)

Lady's Pictorial Magazine, 15 July 1893. *(Author's collection)*

Just as crinolines before them, bustles did not meet with approval in the workplace. In 1888 in Huddersfield an ingenious manager of a shirt factory issued a mandate against the wearing of bustles by his employees and justified his draconian law by the following calculation:

> a girl will arrange her bustle 5 times a day, occupying one minutes time whenever she does so, and that makes a loss of 5 minutes. Where there are 12 girls it means the loss of an hour. Then they will leave the shop 5 times more which takes five minutes each time. That makes 25 minutes or you might say half an hour. 12 girls, each losing half an hour means a loss of 6 hours, added to the bustle hour makes 7. This means a great deal of money when you are paying girls by the week. Taking the bustle-wearing population of London as 1,000,000, the daily loss of time at this rate in London alone is equal to more than 50 years!

There had always been a danger that a bustle/pad or dress improver could become loose, slew around the body and make a lady look decidely lopsided! But as the 1880s slipped into the 1890s the bustle began to fade until only a small pad was left to be replaced by a long-bodied, heavily boned corset. Gwen Raverat, the granddaughter of Charles Darwin, touched upon the realistic discomforts of wearing corsets in her classic memoir of a Cambridgeshire childhood called *Period Piece*, published in the 1950s.

> the ladies never seemed at ease … For their dresses were always made too tight, and the bodices wrinkled laterally from the strain; and their stays showed in a sharp ledge across the middle of their backs. And in spite of whalebone, they were apt to bulge below the waist in front; for, poor dears, they were but human after all, and they had to expand somewhere.

The demise of the bustle necessitated drastic action from an Australian draper, whose story appeared under the heading 'A Sea of Ladies Bustles', reported in the *Liverpool Echo* on 16 June 1893.

> The Melbourne drapers who have large stocks of unsalable bustles on hand are now busy throwing the obsolete feminine adornments into the sea. The only way to recover the import duty paid on them is to re-export so the bustles are exported accordingly and when the vessel gets out to sea they are heaved overboard. The sea is dotted all over with bustles and sometimes they even come ashore.

Once again attention was focused firmly on the waist and from now on it would be the 'S' bend corset that would straddle the decades either side of the twentieth century and set the Edwardian silhouette.

CHAPTER 10

La Belle Époque

'… when Paris seemed to be the artistic center of the universe'
Merriam-Webster Thesaurus

The previous century had produced crinolines, bustles, frills and flounces of every description, but now under a new monarch and a new modern way of thinking Victorian Britain was fading and the belle époque (beautiful era) had arrived. Edward VII's reign was to last just a fraction of his mother's but it had no less impact on the world of fashion. In fact, he and his wife Princess Alexandra had already been influencing fashion for at least a decade, together setting the tone for society which was copied and adapted by those of lower standing and income.

In some areas fashion had slowly been taking notice of the new clothes movements and a new 'tailor made' range of clothing developed to cater for, as the magazine *Punch* put it, the 'New Woman'. A new generation of energetic and active young women who indulged in outdoor pursuits such as cycling and were being employed in an ever wider range of white collar jobs, they embraced the new idea of 'separates', namely a plain 'suit' consisting of a skirt with a jacket-bodice or contrasting shirtwaist or blouse devoid of heavy boning. In addition, the hemlines of all walking skirts in the 1890s rose a full 3in off the ground, creating the 'Rainy Daisy' style, so-named because the hems could now be kept dry on rainy days. The widespread adoption of the blouse was arguably the greatest development in dress in the 1890s. It allowed a more versatile style of dressing – one skirt could be worn with a number of different blouses, suitable for different occasions. It could also be purchased ready-made, as the fit was not as important as that of a bodice.

Yet, as with most fashion, just as something sensible comes along to advance a trend then equally something comes along to counter the advantage. With the 'Tailor-Made' it was the reintroduction of the 'Gigot', better known as the 'Leg o' Mutton' sleeve. These had first made an appearance sixty years previously in the 1830s, when it was more commonly called the 'beret' sleeve' which extended flat from the shoulder and had a downward droop which needed stuffing or steel wires inserted to support it. This new modern adaptation was far more upstanding, beginning as a small puff at the top of the sleeve. Set high on the shoulder in 1892, by 1896 the 'Leg o' Mutton' had reached monstrous proportions projecting confidently upwards and outwards (some say to reflect the growing aggressiveness of women) and needing stiff interlinings to hold a good shape. Perhaps women adopted them because they genuinely liked them; the fact they made one's arms resemble two lamb shanks being purposefully overlooked. It is more probable the sleeves had the effect of alluding to a hand-span waist by way of evening out the shoulders. Another trend, the puffed sleeve, which was a short, three-quarter or full-length arrangement, sometimes called the Bishop sleeve, also had the same waist-slimming effect.

By 1899 the charm of the enormous sleeve was lost and only a slim, tight sleeve remained with a few gathers at the top to hint at its former glory. But not all mourned their passing as it was

A Smart Sealskin Coat. *(Messrs. W. C. Williams.)*

Tailor made separates of the 1890s, *Lady's Pictorial Magazine*, July 1893. *(Author's collection)*

remarked upon by a journalist for the *Wells Journal* that 'some ladies are taking very badly to the newer and tighter sleeves. They have a pinched, impoverished sort of look to the eyes which have so long been accustomed to the breadth and importance of Leg o' Mutton's …'. Taking the opposite view, it was said that there was a general consensus among women that they were only too glad small sleeves had finally taken over as they did not want to go back to the previous monstrosities. The main reason for this being that they could once again rejoice at the ease with which their dress sleeves slid inside their jackets!

As strict Victorian attitudes began to recede the early twentieth century was bowing to common sense and simplicity in fashion and, though details were still elaborate, overtly fussy trimmings and unnatural lines were gradually being abandoned. This trend of simplicity would ultimately be intensified and accelerated by the First World War, which would for the first time in history establish two great principles in women's dress – freedom and convenience. Until then there was still a way to go. Trends may have been changing but dressing in Edwardian times was still something of a rigmarole. The day would begin with a woman choosing what undergarments to wear from the numerous sets of 'lingerie's' comprising day and night chemises, drawers, knickerbockers and petticoats, after which she would be laced into either a straight-front or an 'S' curve corset. Tailored morning garments were probably the day's first choice of garment – a smart blouse and gored skirt perfect for walking, shopping or meeting friends. Returning for lunch would necessitate a second change of clothes, this time into an afternoon dress and by 5pm relief was at hand as she could struggle out of her corset and into a tea-gown, which was generally accepted as a delightful informal affair, often white cotton, extremely comfortable and described in *The Times* of 1912 as 'quite the most becoming garment in which a woman can be arrayed'. A dress 'of intimacy, and not to be worn in crowds', it was the perfect garment for lounging and receiving friends. By 8pm, however, it was time once more to be encased in whalebone, possibly after a change of lingerie (and stockings – cotton for day, and embroidered silk for the evening), and then an evening dress, the degree of ornamentation depending if you were going out or not.

Contrary to popular belief, even those in society did not always relish the constant change of clothing, as many Edwardian memoirs recount. Cynthia Asquith wrote:

A large fraction of our time was spent in changing our clothes … particularly in the winter, when you came down to breakfast ready for church in your 'best dress'. After church you went into tweeds. You always changed again before tea into a 'tea gown' if you possessed

Petit Echo de la Mode, 3 February 1895. *(Author's collection)*

that special creation: the less affluent wore a summer day-frock. Thus a Friday to Monday party meant taking your 'Sunday Best', two tweed coats and skirts, with appropriate shirts, three evening frocks, three garments suitable for tea, your best hat – rows of indoor and outdoor shoes, boots and gaiters, numberless accessories in the way of petticoats, shawls, scarves, ornamental combs and wreathes …

Cynthia was also honest enough to admit at times she detested her clothing, unheard of in a society hostess:

Many of our clothes were far from comfortable or convenient. Country tweeds were long and trammelling. Imagine the discomfort of a walk in the rain in a sodden skirt that wound its wetness round your legs and chapped your ankles. Walking about the London streets trailing clouds of dust was horrid. I once found I had carried into the house a banana skin

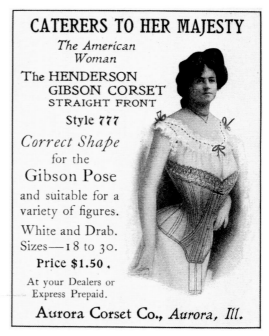

An 'S' bend corset.

The 'S' bend corset managed to contort the female frame into an almost impossible shape.

An advertisement for a 'non-rustable' corset by Bon Ton, 1913.

A corset advertisement from *Good Housekeeping*.

which had got caught up in the hem of my dress. I hated the veils that, worn twisted into a squiggle under my chin, dotted my vision with huge black spots like the symptoms of liver trouble. They flattened even my short eyelashes. Our vast hats which took to the wind like sails were painfully skewered to our heads by huge ornamental hatpins, greatly to the peril of other people's eyes.

Edwardian society revolved around the London Season which ran from February to July, and necessitated a twice-yearly shopping trip to London or, if seriously wealthy, Paris. During the months of March and later in September, droves of women could be seen descending upon shops and fashion houses where a personal *vendeuse* would help them choose six month's worth of wardrobe for the coming season, and seamstresses would work away feverishly in the backrooms.

But none of these outfits would have produced the right effect without the corset of the moment, mentioned previously, the 'S' bend. It differed from the circular wasp-waisted 'swan-bill' corset of the 1890s with its divided bosom, called a 'divorce', and was instead a straight-front corset with an elliptical waist line which forced the torso back into a curve, leaving the breasts pushed forward and unseparated. This created the familiar mono-bosom look of the Edwardian era with this particular corset hailed as being less constricting and more comfortable as well as being able to produce a tiny waist. As a rule of thumb a woman's waist was supposed to measure, before she was married and had children, the same as her age in years! Advice was also at hand from many sources for those whose waists had not returned to a pre-childbearing hand-span and who needed a little help. Bertha Hasbrook wrote:

> For the stout women … corsets will ever be a matter of vast moment. She is dependent upon the corset for whatever grace she has. It can save her from the flabby look she dreads by day in her waking hours and by night in her dreams. It can turn her flesh to a pleasing firmness of contour, something at least stylish if not exactly in accordance with poetic ideals. The wrong corset, on the other hand, will ruin her last change of good looks. It will show her at her very worst, revealing her faults and exaggerating them.
>
> But she must bear in mind this fact: the flesh that is hers cannot be removed by any corset made. If pressed beyond the endurance of Nature in one spot, it is bound to go somewhere. So don't expect to have it vanish at the magic touch of the corset lace. If you reduce your waistline beyond what you have a right to do, the flesh will be forced up and give the appearance of an atrociously large bust. The thing that a corset will do is to hold the flesh firmly in its proper position and prevent its sagging in the manner which is so unpleasant to see.

One can only imagine the comfort such an address would have given the well-endowed!

Sherman's Excelsior corsets supposedly enabled the wearer to be comfortable in every position. Proposing to help form already youthful figures by not 'repressing every charm', it would also hide the 'irregularities' of an older shape so that no 'defects' would be detected. Even a figure considered 'bad' by the corset would seem 'good'. Comfort, health, deceit. What woman could ask for more?

Perhaps it was the function of the huge Edwardian hats to remedy an imbalance of figure. As the bonnet had disappeared in the 1890s, hats gradually grew wider as the era progressed, the 'Merry Widow' hat, of 1907–8, after a play of that name, retaining its popularity until 1914. There is debate as to what actually came first in this matter, the large hat to adorn the hair or the large hair to support the hat. Whichever, it is certain that women's hair certainly contributed

An Edwardian French corset advertisement for 'elegant women', a marvellous undergarment for the tea-gown obtainable from Mme Desbrueres, Maison 'A Jeanne d'Arc', 265, r St Honore, Paris. *(Author's collection)*

Le Journal des Modes. (Author's collection)

Edwardian Actress Lily Elsie in a large hat and high collar. The hat was named after a famous play at the time, *The Merry Widow*. *(Author's collection)*

to the overall hat silhouette and hairdressers created Pompadour supports as bases over which women could build their hair. Combings from hairbrushes were also regularly stored to make up a matted pad or roll called a 'rat' which was pinned in place and over which the top layer of hair was smoothed to create the full luxurious effect.

Hats which looked as if they were merely resting upon an elegant head were in fact anchored fast to a veritable nest of hair with hat pins often up to 13in long. Laws against hat pins of 'excessive length', or the wearing of them without protective stoppers, were proposed if not implemented in London, New York, Hamburg and Berlin as hat-pin-related injuries became common for both the wearer and unsuspecting fellow passengers in crowded places. Hat pins were also popularly regarded as every woman's weapon against the unwanted attentions of hooligans and ill-mannered brutes, giving rise to a risqué music-hall ballad, 'Never Go Walking Out Without Your Hat Pin'.

For modesty's sake women's clothing of this era was as complicated on the inside as it was beautiful on the outside with tapes and ties fastening one item of clothing to another, such as a blouse to a skirt with hooks on the waist to prevent the exposure of any skin should the arms be raised. It was almost a contradiction in terms, however, as the blouses in question were often soft and clinging, elaborate confections of ribbons and chiffon and other gauzy fabrics. The aptly titled 'pneumonia blouse', with its seductive and almost transparent V-shaped yoke at either the front or the back, was considered quite immodest as its tantalising open work showed glimpses of 'delicate' skin. In America it caused more of a stir than in Britain. Whereas here we thought it added to a young woman's irresistible bewitchment and charm and kindly detracted from a mature lady's tell-tale lines, in Massachusetts in 1906 it met with protracted opposition from what was known as the Purity Brigade.

Where skin was allowed to be shown it was usually that of the shoulder, with beautiful evening gowns designed to be wide-necked to better show them off. With shoulders an important focus

'A Martyr to Fashion' – a comic depiction of the hobble skirt. (Author's collection)

It is not clear whether the large coiffures of the ladies gave rise to big hats or that big hats needed to be supported by 'big' hair. *(Author's collection)*

Lady with parrot, a fashion plate from 1910s–20s. *(Author's collection)*

point, advice was on hand to those who relished beauty tips not unlike today where women are told to rub oil into damp skin to retain youthful moisture. Today we would probably not follow the advice of one newspaper, which recommended that after washing the shoulders in hot water we should 'dry very slightly, and while the skin is still moist should rub in a little glycerine and rosewater, and then dust heavily with a good powder. This should be allowed to sink into the skin for a few moments and finally the shoulders should be polished lightly with a clean leather …'. Surely they were confusing a lady's toilette with the rubbing down of a horse!

With the slow but persistent growth of female emancipation and a changing lifestyle that would see the female skirt rise to knee level in 1926, fashion in 1910 would have one last attempt at reining women in and enveloping them in a restricting cocoon – the 'hobble' skirt. This phenomenon is sometimes credited to Paris designer Paul Poiret, who developed dresses on an oriental theme. Others attribute it to Mrs Hart O. Berg, who took an aeroplane flight with Wilbur Wright in 1908. During the flight she tied a rope around her skirt just below the knee to prevent it from blowing around, and failed to remove it immediately on landing causing her to hobble as she walked. In truth, it was more likely to simply be a natural extension of the longer, slimmer skirt that was coming into vogue. Unfortunately, to wear them properly a woman was required to tie a braid around the skirt just under the knees to prevent her from taking too long a stride and tearing the dress, or alternatively wear a loop around each leg underneath the skirt connected by an elasticised band. Many hobble skirts did in fact have slits or hidden pleats which helped a woman to move more freely, but even then it did not suit all woman and one newspaper commented this was because all female bodies were not 'equally harmonious'.

Surprisingly, at first it was a sensation. At the Brook Manufacturing Company in Northampton 1,200 female workers went out on strike as they said there was such a demand for the skirt it could not be manufactured quickly enough, and having been taken off other jobs to concentrate on the 'hobble' they could not make a sufficient wage. Subsequently, the skirt did not last very long as normal, everyday things such as catching a train became difficult. Whenever a train was getting up steam to glide out of the station a stream of frantic girls in hobble skirts would endeavour to catch it, resulting in a marked rise in female unpunctuality at work as trains were often missed. It was banned in Paris due to the accidents it caused. Women fell so often and so awkwardly that arms and legs were broken. Mrs Ethel Hawksley Linley, aged 32, was walking in the country while wearing such a skirt and attempted to climb a stile, fell, broke her ankle and subsequently died in hospital of the shock. The demise of the skirt was commented on when the *Evening Telegraph* and *Daily Post* (Scotland) reported that the old clothes markets have 'thousands of hobble skirts at knock down prices but there are no buyers!'.

CHAPTER 11

The Roaring Twenties

'The present age is the first that has allowed a girl to be a decent percentage of herself …'
Nottingham Evening Post, Saturday, 2 October 1926

It seems unimaginable that women had to wait almost 2,000 years before they felt they could at last be themselves and not simply the clothes they had to wear. The war years of 1914–18 resulted in female liberation, though it was a shame it had taken a catastrophe of world-wide proportions for social blinkers to fall and for women to be recognised as useful and capable human beings. In 1926, in an address called 'The Modern Woman' delivered to the National Council of Women, the speaker, a Mrs Gresswell was delighted to confirm that women were finally realising their worth:

> A girl nowadays is allowed to be about 80% herself. In the Victorian era she was allowed to be about 50% or less. This then is the first age wherein she has not been compelled – by law, custom, convention and so forth – to suppress one half of her true self. What she will be when 100% herself is delightful to anticipate.

In hindsight such hopes appear poignant, especially as we now enjoy the benefits of significant changes, such as job equality and improved birth control, which see today's modern woman possibly now about 99.9 per cent of her true self. Mrs Gresswell continued, 'The girl today is ambitious, courageous and loyal … some retrograde people are dazzled by her, see her as a blurred specimen of humanity and wish she would be content to remain that incomprehensible, subtle thing of sex alone.' She went on to warn, however, that new short

CAPES AND COMFORT.

One of the new cape-coats is an extremely useful possession, particularly to the girl who travels a good deal. Its usefulness is further emphasized by the fact that it is "kind" to almost any type of figure that is not so graceful as it might be, for it covers up a multitude of deficiencies. The coat sketched is of light-weight navy blue rep, trimmed with facings of beige. If, however, you intend to use it primarily for travelling purposes, then you will be wise to have it copied in a light-weight plaid material in shades of brown, fawn and orange, and trim it with facings of plain fawn. A simple little fawn or orange crepe de chine frock should be worn beneath it, and the hat might be of brown, with the little upturned brim of fawn or orange to match the frock. Brown shoes and fawn stockings and gloves would complete a smart travelling outfit.

Southend Pictorial Telegraph, 8 May 1926. *(Author's collection)*

hairstyles did not necessarily mean a woman was modern in mind. An Eton crop, she said, could cover a most un-progressive brain and the length of hair or frock had nothing to do with modernity, 'It is the mind that dates us, not the things casually wrapped around it'. In her opinion, just as there were women who did not resort to cosmetics and cocktails and who were wholly modern in mind, there were equally those whose dress, freedom and abounding health were of the age but whose minds were decidedly blank concerning the larger welfare of their sex:

> The old fashioned flapper … is always recognisable in that she has little or no sex-pride. She may have pride of self, but she has no pride in her womanhood, no belief in its importance, claiming from men not the respect due to an equal but the good natured tolerance one accords to a child. Old fashioned flappers are a small minority daily becoming smaller. The average girl has got rid of this unnatural inferiority complex. Most girls today take the keenest interest in their citizenship and fiercely resent the inequalities which are maintained between the sexes.

For the women attending that address it must have seemed that the days ahead would be unhindered. Probably they had never heard themselves so 'talked-up'. Yet, these new lives they were living in the 'roaring twenties' symbolised by the short skirt, bobbed hair and close-fitting cloche hat did not escape scrutiny nor stereotypical remarks and were examples of just how far women still had to go. *The Times* of 1923 commented that the cloche continues because it is the only shape that fits short hair: 'In youth eccentric hairdressing may pass muster but after forty no woman should change the style of her hair'.

The Cloche … a Statement of Understated Chic

The cloche hat was invented by the Parisian milliner and French fashion designer Caroline Reboux in 1908, and it wasn't long before this small, unassuming fashion accessory, along with the dropped-waist dress, became one of the most recognisable shapes of the 1920s. Due to its deep and fitted shape it was given the name 'cloche' (a French translation of the English word 'bell') and soon hairstyles were being created around it .

The hat became especially popular during the 1920s, and continued to be commonly seen until about 1933. As with many fashions before and since, it did not please everyone. On Saturday, 8 August 1925 the *Bath Chronicle and Weekly Gazette* ran the following warning, citing the modest cloche hat as the latest danger to womankind from articles of clothing:

> The new danger in a woman's attire had been pointed out by the Nottingham city coroner at an inquest on a young girl knocked down by a motor-bus travelling at four or five miles an hour. 'The hats worn by women these days are as bad as blinkers on a horse', he said. 'Women are completely blinded on one side of their faces. I wonder they do not meet with more fatal accidents'.

A cloche hat. *(Author's collection)*

A woman's hair was thought to be her crowning glory and to cut it caused condemnation from almost all walks of life. Edwards' 'Harlene for the Hair' advertising was aggressive, using testimonials from royalty and stars of the Victorian music hall. It claimed that Harlene restored the hair, lengthened it, gave it 'body' and encouraged growth in babies! (Author's collection)

126

The coroner was referring to the latest cloche hats – tight at the neck and fairly wide-brimmed at the front, and popular owing to the smart way they fitted shingled heads.

The effect was to make it impossible for any wearer by a mere turn of the head to see traffic more than 10yd away approaching them at right angles. The tightly fitting brims round the ears deadened the warning sounds of traffic. Later, models were made with the front brims turned up and the ears left free from tight coverings (as reported by the *Daily News*).

For the cloche hat to fit and be a success hair needed to be close to the head, preferably slicked down and, of course, short. The subject of short hair was however a bone of contention between those in favour and those against. It seemed there was no limit to the arguments.

In 1923 the Salvation Army was drawn into the debate when reports from America caused considerable interest in England, due to a young Army captain, Mildred Olson, having been called before her superior officer for cutting her hair short. Representatives in London were asked for their opinions on the matter and though their answers varied they all agreed she should not have done it. One lady officer said that for her part she did not like to see bobbed hair and when her girls had asked her opinion on short hair she had always advised against it. A male captain when questioned admitted that in many cases it might improve the appearance but he would not advise any Salvation Army girl to be so frivolous as to cut her hair short. Another officer added that 'the glory of a woman is her hair and to cut it off is to desecrate it'. Neither did bobbed hair sit well with the Nottingham Board of Guardians with regard to the female nurses at their Bagshot Institution. There, in 1925, they were called to explain themselves over allegations that where female staff had already 'bobbed' their hair they had been ordered to grow it back again!

As early as 1922 there were influential figures speaking out against the modern practice of a woman 'bobbing' her hair. A keen evangelist preacher in Aberdeen, the Revd Nicholson, advised an audience of boys in Belfast that they should never marry a girl with bobbed hair, his reason being that the glory of women was in their hair and the Devil liked her to get it cut off. A fair comment for a man of the cloth who appeared to uphold the scriptures where it states that when a man's hair is long it is his shame but for a woman it is her crowning glory. Unfortunately, he then spoiled it by stating that the only way a woman ought to maintain her nails was on the washboard – possibly a sexist step too far.

A Scottish hairdresser, also of the same mind, placed a statement in the *Tamworth Herald* which read: 'For conscientious reasons, based on the teaching of the Holy Scripture, I have decided to discontinue all ladies hairdressing forthwith and I wish this announcement to save as far as possible those concerned from any inconvenience that may be caused thereby.' As a member of a strict religious body, he obviously held extreme views on the bobbing of women's hair.

Almost universally men, it seemed, did not embrace the new-fangled short styles, with one young man unprepared to compromise. Prompted to take matters into his own hands, though perhaps not face to face, he wrote a note explaining his point of view:

Dear Ivy
I am sorry to write these lines, but I think it best that our friendship should cease altogether and more so now, seeing you have put the lid entirely on, as you have had your hair bobbed. I cannot see that it suits you and also I am against it altogether. You never told me you were going to have it bobbed so take it for granted that we have finished for good.
Walter.

He was obviously not alone, with husbands and boyfriends not afraid to go to great lengths to show their displeasure. The actions of one French gentleman were certainly a warning to all wives who neglected to consult their husbands before visiting the hairdresser. After his wife, Madame Chaplin, had left the marital home because, she alleged, her husband had insulted her after she had had her hair bobbed, Mr Chaplin obtained a deed of separation for desertion. The wife brought in a counter suit but judgement was given against her on the grounds that 'however insulting the epithets used by her husband might have been they were justified by the fact that the wife had her hair shingled (named after the method for tiling roofs which allows tiles to overlap each other) without her husband's permission'. Strong stuff over something as simple as a haircut, but nowhere as dangerous as an incident in Lisbon. Here because a man's daughter had had her hair cut with her mother's consent he decided to murder them! The suicide of a Charles Serlandier was also blamed on the cutting of a woman's hair when he carried out his threat to shoot himself through the heart if his daughters followed the fashion. The 'bob' was even blamed for the death of a lady of 82 who had had her hair cut and was found dead after complaining of the cold.

The knock-on effect of a woman's new-found freedom to cut her hair was also economic, both abroad and at home. Bobbed hair was blamed for unemployment in China where the industry involved in making hair nets was suffering, while hair-pin manufacture also witnessed a slump. London brush-makers claimed that bobbing and shingling the hair had significantly reduced the demand for hair brushes, with one claiming that he had been able to sell dozens in his twenty-two years in the trade but now he was hard-pressed to sell even one. 'Nowadays ladies only need a small pocket comb', he mourned.

Mother and daughter with Marcel waved hair, 1920s/1930s. The style was liberating for women but not universally favoured by men. *(Author's collection)*

Scare stories abounded aimed at changing the minds of those about to follow the new fashion, with statistics released claiming that bobbing, shingling and clipping were causing more premature grey hair among women under 30 than there had ever been before. Hairdressers, disregarding their own profits, even warned their clients that shingling usually meant grey hair in a year, one commenting:

Britain is being turned into a nation of grey-haired young women … women come to me with faces totally unsuited to shingling and ask me to cut their hair for them. I beg them not to but they want me to go ahead. One woman of about 45 with a beautiful classical head insisted on having her head bobbed last week. When she saw the result she burst into tears.

On the whole it did not deter those eager to go ahead and hairdressers could not help but prosper, with no unemployment and London's hairdressers in particular enjoying a period of unparalleled prosperity. A skilful hairdresser earned anything up to £12 a week, with weekly wages, including tips to girl assistants, averaging about £7 in the West End. For the first time in history, a woman having her hair cut in this manner always needed to look well groomed and so frequent visits to her hairdresser were paramount, but in no way an inconvenience. 'Bobbed hair is a state of mind and not merely a new manner of dressing my head' was the statement of one woman interviewed in the *Pictorial Review* of 1927. When she added, 'to my way of thinking, long hair belongs to the age of general feminine helplessness. Bobbed hair belongs to the age of freedom, frankness, and progressiveness', she unwittingly echoed the thoughts in most of the bobbed heads in the country.

The problem of cropped hair did, however, remain a sticking point with the threat of the shingle style even reaching the upper tiers of society and debated in relation to the 'coming-out' of many young debutants who would be taking part in the ceremonies to be held in May and June. As in other years, in 1927 the Lord Chamberlain was to set the rules on how long a train should be, the length of sleeves, etc. and it was rumoured that this year he would be asked by the King to discourage cropped and shingled hair. It was well known that the King had conservative views on the subject of hairdressing, which were shared by most of the female members of the royal family, but he had never sought to impose his views on society in general. It was rumoured that the Duchess of York was contemplating a 'shingle', and someone else had remarked that while Mrs Winston Churchill and other ladies had cut their hair, Mrs Baldwin, and Lady Chamberlain would never sacrifice their tresses.

Josephine Baker popularised the severe Eton crop hairstyle, which did not suit everybody. *(Author's collection)*

'Flapper-girl' designs from the *Ladies' Home Journal*, 1928, claiming to be 'chic in their simplicity'. *(Author's collection)*

If short hair in general was a problem then the particularly short Eton crop style was a catastrophe. Intended to be the ultimate symbol of female liberation, it was modelled on a masculine hairstyle, copying a slicked down appearance with long kiss curls in front of the ears to resemble sideburns. Popularised by Hollywood star Josephine Baker, it was extreme to say the least with Baker's image used to promote a hair pomade called Bakerfix, created by her and which made the style perfect for the cloche hat. Newspapers loved to hate it with headlines such as 'How much longer will the women of England allow their beauty to be mutilated by the Eton Crop?' and 'Hideous Eton Crop – fashion that suits no woman' backed up by Bond Street stylists who damned it as 'ugly' and 'Manish'. Some elements of the media tried to promote a balanced view, one featuring a letter from an employer of numerous girl clerks and typists who said he was pleased with the Eton crop as it made 'the office look neater' and gave the place a more business-like appearance. To trivialise the whole matter it was then dismissed as a summer fancy and would wane in the winter when women, feeling cold, would be only too pleased to grow back their hair.

The Shock of the New

It is fair to say that when ladies' skirts rose after the First World War gentlemen were at a loss as to where to look, so unused were they to seeing – for the first time in public – a woman's ankle. By the 1920s, with cropped hair and the lean boyish silhouette in the form of drop-waisted dresses which flattened the breasts and made no distinction between waist and hips, men had become quite confused. To say that the straight lines of the modern woman's dress were disliked was an understatement, after all for centuries gentlemen had found beauty in a woman's curves, and to have all a woman's charms de-sexualised at once was most disconcerting. The advent of the shorter skirt went some way to redressing the balance but also left many a male embarrassed and unable to believe his eyes.

In 1928 the writer, George Bernard Shaw addressed a public meeting at the King's Theatre, Hammersmith where he, over the course of the evening, expressed many interesting observations made over his lifetime, including the fact that as a man living and working for the most part during the Victorian period he had at an early age formed the opinion that in the matter of dress women were far more 'upholstered' than 'dressed':

> The Victorian age succeeded in one of the most amazing and grotesque enterprises ever tried by mankind. The thought that woman was a human being was intolerable to them. They set up a convention that women were angels. It's all very well being an angel up to a certain point: but there comes a time when you are impressed by the fact that you are not an angel but a human being with a human being's needs. When crinolines were beginning to drop out a lady who was always in advance of her age, suddenly appeared at our house and disclosed what to me was the amazing fact that … women had legs.

Glad the past had faded and the world was embracing new and exciting ideas, he finally declared, 'I can stand any amount of ladies with short skirts nowadays'.

Medical opinion was in full support of the short skirt, advocating the health benefits of no longer having to wear ground-sweeping garments which gathered mud and germs and were a symbol of the sham and gentility of the Victorian era. The short skirt had not only changed the appearance of the wearer but put women on an equal footing with their brothers and introduced them to the advantages of recreation. No longer tied simply to reading books, now they could play tennis, hockey and golf. They could go swimming, dancing and walking and do themselves more physical good in a year than their grandmothers had done in a lifetime. A new found badge of freedom, the short skirt put an end to voluminous clothing and a woman's inability to 'indulge herself in the healing properties of sun and air'.

School medical officers had nothing but praise for the short skirt, reminding those against it how in the past female fashions had sapped a girl's strength and that now female health had greatly improved with the passing of the corset and garters. Even Harley Street doctors praised both short skirts and short hair saying they were two of the greatest boons to modern womanhood. Supposedly, one advantage of short hair was that it reduced headaches and it was advocated that if a woman cut both the length of her skirt and lightened the weight of her lingerie by half, and went out in the cold wearing only two layers of clothing, she would extend her life by at least five years! It was the popular belief that, in short, the short skirt was here to stay.

On the contrary, Paris dress designers were up in arms in 1929 with fashion experts declaring that women's hems must once again descend as 'since the short skirt came into being there has been no "chic" among women'. They pointed out that the skirt had been around for fifteen years now and was a creation of the war years, not a product of France but of the Americans. The French wanted to make women 'charming' again. 'What can one do with it?' French fashion houses decried. 'The short skirt is the uniform of the giddy flapper and we have had enough of it. We want women's fashions to be the fashions of the few. It is impossible to differentiate between women of different rank if they wear short skirts.' This was a clear indication that for some the pre-war class system was not quite dead. 'Dressmaking has taken a battering with the low level the short skirt had reduced it to. People are losing their taste for beautiful fabrics.' Short skirts, however, held out against their critics.

Amendralejo, a town in western Spain, proposed to introduce a tax on women whose dress reached less than a certain minimum length. To ensure the proper observance of the regulations,

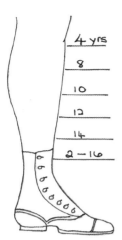

For over two centuries a young girl's skirt length was related to her age. (*Author's collection*)

a tax inspector, provided with a yard measure, was employed to patrol the town and stop every woman whose skirt, according to his view, was not proportionate to the official measurements and if found not to comply the woman was to receive a court prosecution and fixed fee. If she wished she could buy a licence which would enable her to wear the offending skirt and if she renewed it on a monthly basis she could continue to do so. Mill girls in Italy were also threatened with dismissal for having skirts too short as part of an anti-indecent dress crusade, and men urged to end all friendships with women friends whose clothes 'offended their susceptibilities'. In one northern Italian town youths took things into their own hands and seized girls whose knees could be seen, marking with heavy crayon the point on their stockings where it was thought seemly that their skirts should end.

Strangely enough there had always been an unwritten rule as to the length of a girl's skirt as she grew up but with the advent of the short skirt that seemed forgotten, and replaced with the theory that if you measured your ankle and then subtracted that number from twenty your skirt length would best complement your height and shape. Thus if your ankle was 8in, and subtracted from 20in this would leave 12in, the optimum length of your skirt from the floor. Another theory was that instead of the seven ages of man there should be the seven ages of the skirt, with girls in their teens allowed to wear the ultra-short skirt coming just below the knee, with a few inches to be added for each ten years. There would then be a perfect gauge from the ages of 17 to 70.

By November 1926 short skirts were thought a problem in the winter months and a Regent Street firm of shoemakers invented a stocking guard to save silk stockings from being mud-spattered. These were translucent rubber that according to the adverts were 'practically unnoticeable when worn'. They could be slipped on and off in an instant and afforded absolute protection from ankle to knee. Their transparency in no way detracted from the beauty of silk stockings. They were certainly popular as 10,000 pairs were sold by the firm in the first week.

Controversy followed the short skirt (and the girl who was wearing it) wherever it was seen, but for some establishments it was the perfect opportunity to tell the world, or at least the locals, that they were modern and forward thinking as opposed to others who definitely were not. In 1928 Dundee tram officials wanted it known that they had no intention of asking their employees to copy the actions of a neighbouring Sheffield tram conductor when he asked a 20-year-old girl whose short skirt offended two elderly women to leave the tram. They wished it known they were not about to embark upon a puritanical campaign against the abrieviated skirt. On the contrary, it was suggested that perhaps if a girl in a short skirt was employed to sit in the tram on a daily basis then ticket sales would no doubt take a turn for the better.

Sheffield Tram Co., on the other hand, had empowered its conductors to evict from their trams anyone thought to be dressed offensively, and this had been carried out in the case of a chimmney sweep who had got on the tram when in full working clothes. He had been thought to be causing offence and so was asked to leave. The Dundee Tram Co. wished it known that the thought of a girl in a short skirt hardly constituted 'offensive' and announced it in the papers. They ended by saying that they did not consider itself a trustee for public morals and therefore would not be throwing any short-skirted ladies off their vehicles, any time soon.

In an attempt to reintroduce long skirts lobbyists tried long and hard to turn the tide but to no avail, even when it was suggested that men can have 'enough of knees no matter how nice the stockings'.

CHAPTER 12

Abominable Trousers and Rationed Fashion

'*Women in Trousers*, a delightfully feminine regiment'
Worcester Journal, 1939

As early as 1876 women who sought greater emancipation and ventured to wear trousers were the subject of much condemnation and were said to be suffering a 'curious disease that should be treated with the usual methods in use at the best conducted hospitals for the insane', or so said the *New York Times*, 27 May 1876. By the end of the nineteenth century it was deemed acceptable that for ladies pursuing sports or gymnastics it was appropriate to 'dress their legs in separate envelopes of cloth'. By 1911 'harem pants', courtesy of French designer Paul Poiret, were trickling into high fashion and made the cover of *Vogue* magazine in 1913. The First World War also established trousers as a practical and less dangerous alternative to long skirts in the male-oriented workplace. Yet, the adoption by women of masculine fashions was not something that was confined to the twentieth century. As early as the 1600 women wore masculine riding jackets and broad-brimmed hats. Military styling on Regency Spencer jackets took the form of braiding and regimental buttons, and bloomers that appeared in the 1840s and 1850s were worn under knee-length skirts before the tailored skirt suits of the 1860s and 1870s which were modelled on masculine styles.

Trousers for women were really popularised by Chanel in the late 1920s as a leisure garment and cut to be quite baggy, the idea being that they hung in a similar way to a skirt. In the 1930s Hollywood actively promoted trouser wearing, with actresses like Katharine Hepburn and Marlene Dietrich wearing them both on and off the screen, not only singularly but as part of a suit. At first women's trousers were quite 'mannish' made in masculine fabrics with deep turn-ups, and when coupled with a jacket and flat-heeled shoes definitely invoked a masculine outline. At one time this silhouette became so prevalent fashion writers cautioned their readers to approach long-haired 'men' in suits with caution, 'since styles had reached the point where you slap your uncle on the shoulder and it turns out to be your aunt'.

Dresses were by no means side-lined, especially now that skirt lengths had fallen dramatically from the dizzy heights of the 1920s, adding to a new long, lean sophisticated look. Many forward-thinking women viewed trousers as an expression of a new-found confidence. One brave gentleman in 1932 made the statement that he thought the wearing of trousers by women was a symbol of their changed outlook and foreshadowed a time when women would be the superior sex and the dominant partner in human relationships. In hindsight that was nothing short of prophetic.

A 1918 political glamour statement from the Spurgin Women's Suffrage Lecture. *(Author's collection)*

A DEPARTMENT for DAUGHTERS

HERE is news that will bring joy to the hearts of girls and young women trying to make their dress allowance stretch a little further. Marshall & Snelgrove's Debutantes Department features the most attractive and fascinating fashions at excitingly low prices. Printed Silk Frocks from 30/-, Youthful Evening Gowns at 52/6, little Beach and Bungalow Frocks at less than 20/-. These are just a few of the many attractions awaiting you in the Debutantes Department.

ORDER BY POST !

You may order by post with complete confidence. Please state style, size and colour required. All orders are executed by an experienced staff and selections will gladly be sent on approval if desired.

ROUGETTE

Evening Gown in heavy satin, adapted from Lucien Lelong, fashionable revers on bodice and new fullness at back. Colours : white, nil green, ice blue, royal, parchment, dusky pink, nigger, black. **65/-** Sizes : 38, 40, and 42.

Sent on Approval.

The New Debutantes Floor at MARSHALL & SNELGROVE'S
(Debenhams Ltd)
Tel. Mayfair 6600
OXFORD STREET LONDON, W.1.

The lean and slender lines of the 1930s. *(Author's collection)*

'The Lines that Slenderise', *Woman's World*, June 1931. *(Author's collection)*

Being slender was the best way to wear trousers and women were encouraged to adhere to a weight restriction of under 150 pounds (68 kilos) if they wanted to look their best. Despite being favoured by many well-heeled and constantly dieting young women, now able to dress themselves effortlessly, outside Tinsel-Town trouser-wearing in public was far from socially acceptable. A most controversial subject, opinions, judgements and conflicting points of view unravelled almost daily across newspaper columns and the pages of fashion and lifestyle magazines. One such report appears drastic and quite sexist by today's standards when in 1933 two nurses at the Leicester Royal Infirmary were dismissed for wearing men's flannel trousers when off duty! Admittedly, they had been warned by the matron that it was not in keeping with the dignity of the profession or of the hospital. Both voiced their indignation that they should be thus penalised for following fashion when not even at work.

Reports of numbers of young women parading in what were clearly men's ready-made flannel trousers was reported in the *Liverpool Post*, which commented that it was both 'ungainly and vulgar' and that they looked 'horrid'. It comes across to the modern ear all the more shallow and petty when the article added that 'Some men hold the opinion that a beautiful woman should still look beautiful whatever she wore; some of the modern young men however do not include trousers in this category.'

The idea held by the male half of the population that women in trousers had the propensity to be 'troublesome' was reiterated when in 1936 a master of Trinity College, Cambridge suggested wearing trousers and smoking cigarettes amounted to the same thing, namely a threat and abomination. Having noticed that the proportion of non-smokers to smokers had noticeably increased

The 1930s' movie star Marlene Dietrich in her 'mannish' suit. *(Author's collection)*

at the college in recent months, he put it down to 'antagonism of the sexes'. In his words, since 'copycat female undergraduates' had taken up smoking and so 'mimicked the superior sex' the men at the university, afraid of appearing 'as effeminate as to puff on cigarettes like mere women', had given up. He then added that if the fashion for women to wear trousers ever extended to the college, men 'in order to preserve the difference between the sexes will be driven to wearing kilts!'.

The blatant dislike of women upsetting the natural order of things was obvious in an exchange in the *Hull Daily Mail* in 1936, when a Bradford girl defendant astonished the local magistrates by appearing before them wearing grey flannel trousers. She had been summoned for using a motor vehicle without appropriate insurance and when called forward was asked her name.

'Mary', she replied to which the judge, noting the trousers and short hair, quipped, 'Are you sure?'

With Hollywood fronting the trouser trend it was only a matter of time before an interview with an American actress appeared in a British newspaper. A publication called the *Citizen* asked the legendary actress Marlene Dietrich, 'the epitome of femininity on the screen' among other things, why she liked to wear trousers considering all the controversy. She apparently defended wearing the 'mannish' fashion by saying she thought them both 'warm and comfortable'; it was less expensive to look smart in trousers than in a gown and finished by saying that as she pleased film directors and producers by wearing frills and flounces on set, why should she not please herself once out of the public eye? Three fair points all of which sound perfectly rational!

With the advent of war in 1939 the controversy surrounding trousers temporarily shifted as they became – just as in 1914 – acceptable for women to wear for war work. In March 1941 Ernest Bevin, Minister for Labour, called on the women of Britain to help the war effort, and many not only took new jobs in the munitions factories, but also worked in tank and aircraft factories, drove trains and tractors and operated cranes. Extravagant clothing was ousted by trousers or dungarees and scarves tied around the head to stop hair becoming trapped in machinery. German air raids also made trousers for women a necessity at this time with the 'siren suit' considered the first real 'fashion' item of the war.

This all-in-one boiler suit style first originated in the First World War as practical clothing for munitions workers. The 1940s' styles were usually hooded and had capacious pockets to hold as many objects as possible, given that time was of the essence when leaving your house in a raid. Similarly, they needed to be quick and easy to put on, over night clothes or pyjamas. It was also vital that they were practical to protect against the inhospitable environment of the air-raid shelter, which could have been either a dug-out (Anderson shelter) in the garden or a public shelter such as an Underground station. They were, by all accounts, probably the first and equally the most unlikely fashion garment of the war.

Yet it was not Britain's first experience of 'crisis' clothes. The origins lay in a comparable disaster 200 years earlier when a series of earthquakes threatened to crush Georgian London from beneath just as air raids were about to obliterate the twentieth-century capital from above. Letters from Sir Horace Walpole written from March to April 1750 served to convey the phenomenon, stating that 'within these three days seven hundred and thirty coaches have been counted fleeing past Hyde Park corner, from the alarming effects …' and that with the possibility of further tremors London would have been swallowed up. Walpole advises there was little to be done, though one enterprising young man did sell pills which he claimed were very good against an earthquake, and when London was in the grip of a 'shivering fit' women donned 'earthquake gowns'. Simply made and of functional fabrics, these were to protect themselves against the cold night air, mud and damp as they sheltered on the heights of Hampstead and other 'safe country spots' for fear of being trapped inside their houses should they have collapsed. With two earthquakes already having taken place in the preceding months the old superstition that things happened in threes abounded, just as it did in 1940 where people were trying to predict the exact date of an all-out German invasion. Even air-raid shelters were nothing new. Their equivalent had already been invented in the reign of James I, who, having a morbid fear of fog, ordered the erection of small buildings complete with seats and the facilities for a fire for those caught out in bad weather to take shelter.

The siren suit even had royal patronage as Princesses Elizabeth (the future Queen Elizabeth II) and her sister Margaret both owned one, as did Winston Churchill who, preferring to call it his 'romper suit', caused a media stir when he wore his travelling from Boston to New York on war business.

Even when prompted by a global crisis, for some, women in trousers was still unthinkable. On 3 October 1939 the *Dundee Courier* reported how a Middlesbrough magistrate, as part of

Trousers, or the boiler suit, worn by munitions workers in the First World War re-appeared in the Second World War. *(Author's collection)*

Trousers were worn for war work in both world wars. From *WW1 Women at War – the Munitions Factory*. *(Author's collection)*

The practical 'siren suit' of the Second World War years. *(Author's collection)*

clarifying an item mentioned in his case, asked in court, 'What is a woman's Siren suit? Is it a suit that women wear after the siren has gone or a suit which makes them look like a siren?' The resulting comment from his clerk, 'It is just a woman's excuse to wear trousers!', was to the point, sexist and blatantly condescending.

The siren suit was a success and sold even after the immediate threat of air raids had passed. The store D.H. Evans marketed them as a practical and common-sense garment and advertised 'a fashionable, wool, zip fronted siren suit, with belt, cuffs, hood and pockets all in cobalt blue for only forty five shillings and sixpence'. This wartime phenomenon did much to establish trousers for women, but they remained a gender specific garment in the eyes of men, with critics still considering it 'improper to indicate the shape of a woman's leg with trousers'. One editor of a women's magazine aired her views by saying that she believed 'trousers simply will not be around in the future as men do not like them'. In hindsight, a slight faux pas on her part?

In 1942, however, trade experts announced that more women would adopt trousers due to the shortage of suspenders, which was a direct result of a lack of rubber, which in turn was no longer allowed in the manufacture of girdles. Women were going bare-legged, even if stockings were available. In America women were asked to give up the stockings they did have by taking them to collection points displaying signs that read 'Uncle Sam needs your silk or nylon stockings for gun-powder bags and parachutes'. They had already given up their girdles to save on rubber and now each parachute needed at least thirty-six pairs of stockings.

If a woman could not go completely bare-legged then, on both sides of the Atlantic she was encouraged to wear ankle socks instead. This was no mean feat as for centuries women's legs had been covered and even as late as 1934, only five years before the war, it was commonly thought that 'Few women possess limbs so perfect that they can be extravagant in the freedom afforded to legs …', and that without stockings an 'ensemble' is not finished off, as reported in the *Gloucestershire Echo*, Wednesday, 16 May 1934. In short, wearing stockings made a woman well groomed and, according to the article, 'assisted a woman to a sublime state of mind'.

When, in reality, it is doubtful that any women would de-stabilise the war effort simply to appease her state of mind, the lack of stockings was particularly hard to assimilate. In 1942, however, one newspaper was pleased to announce that at least one English county had an answer to the stocking problem. It appeared that 'depots' were shortly to open where women could take old stockings to be re-heeled and re-soled with salvaged materials which had been cleaned and sterilised. A wide range of shades was available in large quantities so it was possible to effect a suitable match. The charge for silk stockings would be 2 shillings and 6 pence. No coupons were needed for such mending. Fortunate for some. However, not to be thwarted by location, those women still wishing to appear well groomed and not living in the county in question turned to gravy browning and a good friend who could draw, with an eyebrow pencil, a good straight line as a stocking seam down the back of their leg. If all else failed, befriending a black marketer or a visiting GI could get you a regular supply.

One of the most unusual items affected by the war was women's stockings. With an embargo on Japanese silk, nylon was promptly drafted to make parachutes. *(Library of Congress)*

On Whit Sunday, 1 June 1941 strict clothes rationing was introduced with the following announcement:

> Rationing has been introduced not to deprive you of your real needs, but to make more certain that you get your share of the country's goods – to get fair shares with everybody else. When the shops re-open you will be able to buy cloth, clothes, footwear and knitting wool only if you bring your food ration book with you. You will have a total of 66 coupons to last you a year; so go sparingly. You can buy where you like and when you like without registering.

This strategy was severe and took the population from being used to 'plenty' straight to 'hard to come by' and by pre-war standards such an allowance would have been spent in the first quarter of any year. By 1942 this allowance had dropped to forty-eight coupons. Each page of coupons was a different colour to stop people using up all their coupons at once. People were only allowed to use one colour at a time, with the government telling people when they could start using a new colour. The coupon system allowed people to buy one completely new set of clothes once a year. By 1945 clothing coupons were as low as thirty-six a year and inevitably a black market in coupons sprang up and vast numbers of books, about 700,000, were lost or stolen in the early stages of the scheme.

The Allocation of Clothing Coupons for Males, 1941

Item of Clothing	Adult	Child
Pair of Socks or Stockings	3	1
Pair of Boots or Shoes	7	3
Nightshirt or Pair of Pyjamas	8	6
Raincoat or Overcoat	16	11
Waistcoat, or Pull-over, or Cardigan or Jersey	5	3
Trousers (other than Fustian or Corduroy)	8	6
Fustian or Corduroy Trousers	5	5
Shorts	5	3
Dressing Gown or Bathing Gown	8	6
Shirt, or Combinations – Woollen	8	6
Shirt, or Combinations – Other Materials	5	4

The Allocation of Clothing Coupons for Females, 1941

Item of Clothing	Adult	Child
Lined Mackintoshes or coats (over 28in long)	14	11
Jacket or Short Coat (under 28in long)	11	8
Dress or Gown or Frock – Woollen	11	8
Dress or Gown or Frock – Other Material	7	5
Blouse or Sports Shirt, or Cardigan, or Jumper	5	3
Skirt or Divided Skirt	7	5
Apron or Pinafore	3	2
Pyjamas	8	6
Nightdress	6	5
Pair of Stockings	2	1
Pair of Socks (ankle length)	1	1

There were items that could be bought without coupons such as clothing and sundries for babies under 4 months old, as well as overalls, hats and caps, sewing thread, mending wools and silks and shoe and boot laces. Also exempt were braids, ribbons and other fabrics less than 3in in width, elastic, lace, braces, suspenders, garters, clogs and black-out dyed cloth. Coupons were not needed for second-hand articles. The scheme continued to issue coupons until 1949, with all forms of rationing ending in 1952.

As well as the coupon system a utility or austerity scheme was introduced by the British Board of Trade, making sure that both low and medium quality consumer goods were produced at reasonable prices and to high standards, while also meeting the restrictions on raw materials and the freeing up of labour to work on more important considerations. This clothing carried the label CC41. Regulations affected the style and design of clothing and for women there was a limit on the number of pleats, buttonholes, pockets and seams items could have. There was a maximum width for sleeves, belts and collars. Seams themselves had to be narrow and hem length strictly regulated. Women were only allowed four buttons per coat. Men too had their extras cut. Shirts were much shorter in length, and no longer had double cuffs. Trousers had no turn-ups, jackets ceased to be double-breasted and pockets no longer had covering flaps. Such small things apparently, though insignificant, all added up. The 2in saved from the bottom of shirts and the changing of double to single cuffs on the sleeves saved 4 million square yards of cotton per year and freed up 1,000 workers from clothes factories enabling them to join the war effort. Similarly, embroidery, and special finishing in leather and fur trimmings, disappeared on outer wear altogether. All women were encouraged to polish up their sewing skills with easy dress and style templates produced in a number of limited but stylish designs. The female silhouette became refined and unadorned, her minimal but versatile wardrobe made up of short straight skirts and boxy jackets with shoulder pads. Yet in spite of its austere specification, utility clothing designs were commissioned from leading fashion designers including Hardy Amies, Norman Hartnell and other members of the Incorporated Society of London Fashion Designers.

To tap into patriotism media campaigns were launched with a character named 'Mrs Sew & Sew' and the slogan 'Make Do and Mend' became a familiar mantra. The need to conserve every scrap of material in the country was of the utmost importance and universally discussed at

Wartime utility fashion advertising card. Buttons and pockets were reduced in numbers as was the amount of fabric allowed to be used in making any garment. Utility Model No. 424 claimed to be 'superbly tailored in fine, smooth, two-tone tweed'. *(Author's collection)*

HOUSEWIFE'S GUIDE TO MAKING & MENDING

6D

A 1940s wartime housewife's guide to making and mending. *(Author's collection)*

council chamber meetings, which were charged with investigating ways of extending the scope of the 'Make Do and Mend' campaign. It was recognised that the voluntary services would be invaluable in providing information and in the provision of demonstrations. In addition, 'Make Do and Mend' centres, usually village halls, would employ a resident dressmaker to help with alterations and repairs. It was even proposed by some school superintendents that in order to take some of the burden off their mothers, pupils who were old enough should be allowed to bring clothes into school and carry out repairs themselves under supervision. Many schools also acted as clothes exchanges, where garments could be donated that did not require alteration.

On 1 September 1943 *The Times* launched the Board of Trade's booklet 'Make Do and Mend', which at a cost of 3 pence was a sound investment in the campaign to make clothes last longer in compliance with the war effort. *The Times* stressed that the booklet would 'make rationing more tolerable' as it contained practical hints, some no doubt already known to housewives but included many new ones necessitated by the circumstances. One section, 'men's clothes into women's', was especially mentioned, with the paper quoting, 'Here are some ways in which a man's unwanted garments can be converted to your own use …', but stressed the woman should be 'quite sure he won't want them again after the war!'. It also had practical answers to the age-old moth problem that had blighted clothes from time immemorial.

Pillowcases were made into white shorts for summer, skirts were made from men's old trousers and cast-offs expertly fashioned into children's clothes. Collars would be added and trims applied all to eke out a limited wardrobe. Wedding dresses would be worn several times, borrowed by sisters and friends, until through necessity they had to be recycled into underwear or nightgowns. Blankets were used to make coats. The wedge shoe, first designed by Salvatore Ferragamo in 1936 from cork and wood, was practical, cheap and sturdy, lasting a long time and needing minimal repair.

CHAPTER 13

Cinched and Pinched – *A Brave New World?*

'Bravo! Magnifique! Ravissant!'
Reaction to Christian Dior's 'New Look', Paris 1947

In 1947, two years after the war ended, the fashion pendulum swung once more, this time out of grey and grim wartime austerity towards an ultra-feminine 'new look', a phrase coined by Carmel Snow, editor of American *Harper's Bazaar*, and designed by Frenchman Christian Dior. Though trousers were accepted in the workplace and for leisure, dresses and skirts were still considered proper garments for going out in public and Dior's creations once again celebrated the hour-glass shape with London couturier John Cavanagh describing the style as 'a total glorification of the female form, all waist, hip and breast'.

No doubt a breath of fresh air for those tired of the military, masculine look, this latest phenomenon was a direct backlash as skirts now sported yards and yards of fabric. But with few women actually possessing a perfect hour-glass shape and designers willing to contort what she had to fit his ideal, yes, you've guessed correctly, a voluminous petticoat, in essence a crinoline, was re-introduced to flare out the hips under the skirt aided by a 'cincher', if not a full corset, employed to reduce the waist. If that is not a fashion full circle then what is?

Dior was heavily criticised for his innovation as the amount of fabric required to create a New Look garment was in direct conflict with the rationing that was still in place. With the economic situation in Britain remaining dire, opposition to the New Look was based on 'waste'. Things even reached the ears of the Board of Trade when an English fashion journalist, Alison Settle, went to see Sir Stafford Cripps, its President. Intent on getting the clothing ration increased in order for women to be able to afford even one New Look dress, she was greeted instead with a bellowed 'out of the question'. With England struggling to get back on its feet, Cripps was astounded women would even consider buying something that would far outstrip their coupons. He even suggested there should be a law against the 'Look' and its swaying ballerina skirts which swirled around the legs held out by taffeta and tulle petticoats.

The New Look also cinched and pinched women into shapes reminiscent of those of their Victorian if not Georgian grandmothers. Rob Wagner, an article writer for the American publication the *Script*, in May 1947 wrote disparagingly of Dior's revolution in women's dress, saying it tried to make a woman look good 'where she aint'. Others, especially older women who well remembered the sacrifices made in the 'Make Do and Mend' years, were having none of it. In autumn 1948 a photographer captured on film an incident in the Parisian Rue Lepic where a young woman literally had her clothes torn off by outraged females who were incensed at the yards of fabric in her new skirt.

Christian Dior's 'New Look' of 1947 was a world away from the austere fashions of the war years.

It was hard for English women to see the French and American fashion markets at liberty to indulge in Dior's generous designs given that they were still at the mercy of rationing. However, it wasn't long before a forward-thinking buyer for a chain of low-price clothes shops managed to supply outlets with racks of inexpensive copies of 'New Look' clothes. Suddenly, like so many amiable sheep, English women were able to follow their transatlantic sisters and indulged for the first time in a decade in feminine contours, broader hiplines and smaller waists. It was not easy as a stodgy wartime diet would now make it necessary for most English women to slim-down in order to wear them properly. Dior's designs, reminiscent of those created by bustles and crinolines, required an average 20in waist, which even models were finding difficult to maintain. For one fashion show where the modelling was to have been shared between American and French mannequins it was eventually decided that only the French women were to be used as the American waistline averaged 25in.

The hand-span waist so beloved by Dior was achieved by a waist cincher. Popularly called the 'waspie' or 'guepiere', it was boned and back-laced, and differed from the Victorian corsets of the previous century only in length, usually being a narrow 6 to 7in and used not whalebone but what magazines of the day liked to call 'super-light-weight feather boning'.

'I think of my work as ephemeral architecture, dedicated to the beauty of the female body', Dior.

It was also a godsend for Dior that the young English princesses, daughters of King George VI, Elizabeth and Margaret were captivated by the New Look, but despite their 'captivation' the King still insisted they comply with the restrictions of the day just as everyone else. Fortunately, a royal courtier managed to give Princess Margaret a taste of the New Look she wanted by having one of her coats altered within the proper limits by the insertion of several black velvet bands and so was able to afford the princess the desired silhouette. By the autumn of 1947 when Dior was showing his collection at the Savoy a request was made by the Palace for a private viewing of his collection in the presence of the Princesses Elizabeth and Margaret and their mother the Queen. Also in attendance would be the Duchess of Kent and her sister, Princess Olga of Yugoslavia. A slightly clandestine affair, the venue was to be the home of the French ambassador's wife, Madame Massagli, into which dresses and models were smuggled with the minimum of publicity. Four years later Dior had obviously found royal approval as he was commissioned to design Princess Margaret's ball gown on the occasion of her 21st birthday in 1951.

Dior went from strength to strength but denied he had worked any miracles. 'No one person can change fashion – a big fashion change imposes itself', he declared, adding, 'the New Look was inevitable because women longed to look like women again'. Dior had read the mood of the world's women and got it right, but also re-introduced the tyranny of previous centuries where women were obliged to fit their clothes as opposed to their clothes fitting them. To get the fashion right magazines became full of adverts for girdles, cinchers, corsets and 'corselets', unwittingly advocating today's modern adage of 'no pain no gain' with slogans such as 'To maintain your figure at its flattering best, depend on foundation garments to control and distribute' or 'your

'You can wear yours all day with ease … your hips prettily curved, your waist incredibly tiny … precisely the figure that fashion decrees!'. An advert from 1948 featuring both a long-line girdle and wasp-waist or 'waspie' cincher.

figure is moulded into new lines, inches disappear from waist, hips and thighs all with ease and comfort!'. In the light of modern-day fashions it all sounds tantamount to medieval torture, the latter slogan continuing to describe how it was designed with a 'magic double diagonal pull', a double elastic waistband which was wrapped around the waistline and hooked at the back.

With fashion still bullying its way through the post-war decade, what to wear for most was still more of a 'must' than an option. Yet, there was change ahead. The 1950s gave birth to the concept of the teenager, something up until then unheard of. Young people, influenced by film, television, magazines and the music scene, had money in their pockets from paid work and as new consumers were able to fund their independence and indulge in their own style of clothes. No self-respecting 'teen' was content to be a simple miniature of their parents; a new phenomenon, 'The Generation Gap', had well and truly arrived.

With the 1960s emerging as a decade of growing optimism and social and economic change fashion completely shrugged off structured styles, embracing instead a vibrant youth culture and young people's tastes in clothes followed their taste in music. Short A-line styles in bright colours were sold cheaply in London boutiques and inspirational new designers experimented with geometric shapes, new textiles and patterns with Mary Quant ultimately popularising the 'mini-skirt' which sat well over 7in above the knee. It was an iconic garment, one that possibly paralleled the boyish 'flapper' style in vogue in the 1920s and though nearly half a century apart both styles screamed liberation.

While it was a short-lived freedom for the flapper, youth was not about to relinquish its hold on the fashion world so quickly a second time and can be seen behind almost every fashion trend from then until the present day. With mini-skirts and hot-pants exposing ever more flesh and fronting what appeared to many to be a total abandonment of decency, hemlines, in 1970, suddenly plummeted as ladies voluntarily adopted a new ankle-length maxi-skirt with enthusiasm. Was this, in retrospect, a defining decision? Was this

The mini-skirt hits London, 1960s. *(Photograph Robert Hallmann)*

fashionable return to modesty the pivotal moment women stopped being slaves to fashion and had the final say in how they looked? One could argue that if it wasn't for the designer swinging the pendulum yet again women would have had no such choice. Yet, it was more important than

The midi/maxi fashion that followed the mini-skirt.

women today realise. The mere co-existence of the 'long' and 'short' at that particular same moment in time broke all the rules: rules that medieval sumptuary laws and Elizabethan fashion legislation had failed to enforce. From that point on fashion became personal with designers providing the ability to embrace both formality and 'casual dressing', something that has laid the foundations for what we comfortably wear today and how we will be dressed in the future. At last what they wore and how they wore it had become a decision both men and women were finally at liberty to make for themselves.

Conclusion

The fashion wheel never has nor ever will stop turning. The 1980s gave us an economic boom which allowed women willingly to express themselves once more with pseudo-Georgian 'big hair' and the shoulder pads of 'power dressing', while the 1990s and 'Noughties' saw women come back down to earth in a backlash of elegance. Where our third millennia of fashion will take us is an adventure about to unfold. What is almost certain is that women will no longer be, in the words of Mrs Gresswell in 1926, 'compelled – by law, custom, convention and so forth' to be defined solely by her clothes.

Endnote

As the author of this book I have discovered a wealth of information on costume and attitudes towards clothing during my research, but my favourite is a 'snippet' that answered a question I have not up until now been able to answer. I have often wondered why almost every bra I have ever owned, no matter what design or brand, has a small bow stitched to the front between the cups. The question was finally answered by the discovery that in the sixteenth and seventeenth centuries when stomachers or 'stay busks' were used to slip down the front of a corset a small piece of ribbon was attached to the top to help remove it easily. Our little ribbon-bows are a direct link to those times, though now purely for decoration. It is a reminder that no matter how uncomfortable our undergarments seem to us today, they were far more uncomfortable and restricting in the past!

APPENDIX

For Your Entertainment

Research for this book has thrown up a surplus of interesting facts, some of which are shared here, for your amusement.

Sumptuary Laws from the Statutes of King Henry VIII and Queen Mary I

For Him … – None shall wear in his apparel:
Any silk of the colour of purple, cloth of gold tissued, nor fur of sables, but only the King, Queen, King's mother, children, brethren, and sisters, uncles and aunts; and except dukes, marquises, and earls, who may wear the same in doublets, jerkins, linings of cloaks, gowns, and hose; and those of the Garter, purple in mantles only.

Cloth of gold, silver, tinseled satin, silk, or cloth mixed or embroidered with any gold or silver: except all degrees above viscounts, and viscounts, barons, and other persons of like degree, in doublets, jerkins, linings of cloaks, gowns, and hose.

Woolen cloth made out of the realm, but in caps only; velvet, crimson, or scarlet; furs, black genets, lucerns; embroidery or tailor's work having gold or silver or pearl therein: except dukes, marquises, earls, and their children, viscounts, barons, and knights being companions of the Garter, or any person being of the Privy Council.

Velvet in gowns, coats, or other uttermost garments; fur of leopards; embroidery with any silk: except men of the degrees above mentioned, barons' sons, knights and gentlemen in ordinary office attendant upon her majesty's person, and such as have been employed in embassages to foreign princes.

Caps, hats, hatbands, capbands, garters, or boothose trimmed with gold or silver or pearl; silk netherstocks; enameled chains, buttons, aglets: except men of the degrees above mentioned, the gentlemen attending upon the Queen's person in her highness's Privy chamber or in the office of cupbearer, carver, sewer [server], esquire for the body, gentlemen ushers, or esquires of the stable.

Satin, damask, silk, camlet, or taffeta in gown, coat, hose, or uppermost garments; fur whereof the kind groweth not in the Queen's dominions, except foins, grey genets, and budge: except the degrees and persons above mentioned, and men that may dispend £100 by the year, and so valued in the subsidy book.

Hat, bonnet, girdle, scabbards of swords, daggers, etc.; shoes and pantofles of velvet: except the degrees and persons above names and the son and heir apparent of a knight.

Silk other than satin, damask, taffeta, camlet, in doublets; and sarcanet, camlet, or taffeta in facing of gowns and cloaks, and in coats, jackets, jerkins, coifs, purses being not of the color scarlet, crimson, or blue; fur of foins, grey genets, or other as the like groweth not in the Queen's dominions: except men of the degrees and persons above mentioned, son of a knight, or son and heir apparent of a man of 300 marks land by the year, so valued in the subsidy books, and men that may dispend £40 by the year, so valued ut supra.

None shall wear spurs, swords, rapiers, daggers, skeans, woodknives, or hangers, buckles or girdles, gilt, silvered or damasked: except knights and barons' sons, and others of higher degree or place, and gentlemen in ordinary office attendant upon the Queen's majesty's person; which gentlemen so attendant may wear all the premises saving gilt, silvered, or damasked spurs.

None shall wear in their trappings or harness of their horse any studs, buckles, or other garniture gilt, silvered, or damasked; nor stirrups gilt, silvered, or damasked; nor any velvet in saddles or horse trappers: except the persons next before mentioned and others of higher degree, and gentlemen in ordinary, ut supra.

Note that the Lord Chancellor, Treasurer, President of the council, Privy Seal, may wear any velvet, satin, or other silks except purple, and furs black except black genets.

These may wear as they have heretofore used, viz. any of the King's council, justices of either bench, Barons of the Exchequer, Master of the Rolls, sergeants at law, Masters of the Chancery, of the Queen's council, apprentices of law, physicians of the King, queen, and Prince, mayors and other head officers of any towns corporate, Barons of the Five Ports, except velvet, damask, [or] satin of the color crimson, violet, purple, blue.

Note that her majesty's meaning is not, by this order, to forbid in any person the wearing of silk buttons, the facing of coats, cloaks, hats and caps, for comeliness only, with taffeta, velvet, or other silk, as is commonly used.

Note also that the meaning of this order is not to prohibit a servant from wearing any cognizance of his master, or henchmen, heralds, pursuivants at arms; runners at jousts, tourneys, or such martial feats, and such as wear apparel given them by the Queen, and such as shall have license from the Queen for the same.

For Her … None shall wear:
Any cloth of gold, tissue, nor fur of sables: except duchesses, marquises, and countesses in their gowns, kirtles, partlets, and sleeves; cloth of gold, silver, tinseled satin, silk, or cloth mixed or embroidered with gold or silver or pearl, saving silk mixed with gold or silver in linings of cowls, partlets, and sleeves: except all degrees above viscountesses, and viscountesses, baronesses, and other personages of like degrees in their kirtles and sleeves.

Velvet (crimson, carnation); furs (black genets, lucerns); embroidery or passment lace of gold or silver: except all degrees above mentioned, the wives of knights of the Garter and of the Privy Council, the ladies and gentlewomen of the privy chamber and bedchamber, and maids of honor.

None shall wear any velvet in gowns, furs of leopards, embroidery of silk: except the degrees and persons above mentioned, the wives of barons' sons, or of knights.

Cowls, sleeves, partlets, and linings, trimmed with spangles or pearls of gold, silver, or pearl; cowls of gold or silver, or of silk mixed with gold or silver: except the degrees and persons above mentioned; and trimmed with pearl, none under the degree of baroness or like degrees.

Enameled chains, buttons, aglets, and borders: except the degrees before mentioned.

Satin, damask, or tufted taffeta in gowns, kirtles, or velvet in kirtles; fur whereof the kind groweth not within the Queen's dominions, except foins, grey genets, bodge, and wolf: except the degrees and persons above mentioned, or the wives of those that may dispend £100 by the year and so valued in the subsidy book.

Gowns of silk grosgrain, doubled sarcenet, camlet, or taffeta, or kirtles of satin or damask: except the degrees and persons above mentioned, and the wives of the sons and heirs of knights, and the daughters of knights, and of such as may dispend 300 marks by the year so valued ut supra, and the wives of those that may dispend £40 by the year.

Gentlewomen attendant upon duchesses, marquises, countesses may wear, in their liveries given them by their mistresses, as the wives of those that may dispend £100 by the year and are so valued ut supra.

None shall wear any velvet, tufted taffeta, satin, or any gold or silver in their petticoats: except wives of barons, knights of the order, or councilors' ladies, and gentlewomen of the privy chamber and bed chamber, and the maids of honor.

Damask, taffeta, or other silk in their petticoats: except knights' daughters and such as be matched with them in the former article, who shall not wear a guard of any silk upon their petticoats.

Velvet, tufted taffeta, satin, nor any gold or silver in any cloak or safeguard: except the wives of barons, knights of the order, or councilor's ladies and gentlewomen of the privy chamber and bedchamber, and maids of honour, and the degrees above them.

Damask, taffeta, or other silk in any cloak or safeguard: except knights' wives, and the degrees and persons above mentioned.

No persons under the degrees above specified shall wear any guard or welt of silk upon any petticoat, cloak, or safeguard.

Elizabethan Recipes for Hair Dye

To colour a blacke haire presently into a Chestnut colour … This is done with oyle of Vitrioll: but, you must doe it verie carefully not touching the skin.

To colour oneself Blonde … Take a pound of finely pulverized beech-wood shavings, half a pound of box-wood shavings, four ounces of fresh liquorice, a similar amount of very yellow, dried lime peel, four ounces each of swallow wort and yellow poppy seeds, two ounces of the leaves and flowers of glaucus, a herb which grows in Syria and is akin to a poppy, half an ounce of saffron and half a pound of paste made from finely ground wheat flour. Put everything into a lye made with sieved wood ashes, bring it partly to the boil and then strain the whole mixture. Now take a large earthenware pot and bore ten or twelve holes in the bottom. Next take equal parts of vine ash and sieved wood ash, shake them into a large wooden vessel or mortar, whichever you think better, moisten them with the said lye, thoroughly pulverize the mixture, taking almost a whole day to do this but make sure that it becomes a bit stiff. Next pound rye and wheat straw in with it until the straw has absorbed the greater part of the lye. Shake these pounded ashes into the said earthenware pot and push an ear of rye into each small hole. Put the straw and ashes in the bottom so that the pot is filled, though still leaving sufficient space for the remainder of the lye to be poured over the mixture. Towards evening set up another earthenware pot and let the lye run into it through the holes with the ears of rye. When you want to use the lotion, take the liquid which ran out, smear your hair with it and let it dry. Within three or four days the hair will look as yellow as if it were golden ducats. However, before you use it wash your head with a good lye, because if it were greasy and dirty it would not take the colour so well. You should note that this preparation will last for a year or two and, if one goes about it properly it can help ten or twelve member of the fairer sex, for very few things will colour the hair.

To Make Ceruse or White Lead Make-up

Take leaden plates, and suspend them over the vapour of very strong vinegar in a vase, which after being heated must be placed in dung for two months; then scrape away the matter that you will find upon the plates, which is the white lead. Do this until the plates are consumed …

Segreti de Colori, fifteenth century

Stuart Wisdom

A Pale Complexion …
Make a cream from powdered white chalk or white lead, mixed with white of egg and vinegar. This makes a smooth shiny finish and but be careful not to laugh least your new 'skin' should crack.

To soften the skin …
Wash in your own urine, or with rosewater mixed with wine, else make a decoction of the rinds of lemon.

Victorian Beauty?

White Arsenic Face Cream – side effects: headaches, confusion, severe diarrhoea, and drowsiness, vomiting, blood in the urine, cramping muscles, hair loss, stomach pain and convulsions.

Cocaine Tooth Paste – side effects: anxiety, irritability, paranoia, damage to heart, brain, lungs, gastrointestinal tract and kidneys.

Deadly Nightshade Eye Drops – side effects: headache, dizziness, anxiety, sensitivity to light, light-headedness, fatigue, blurred vision, nausea and reduced sweating.

Face lotion – Boil some crumb of bread and roots of mallow in filtered rain-water. When the water is a little reduced, strain it through a clean white cloth, then add a good proportion of yolk of egg and some fresh cream. Stir it well, and perfume it with orange-flower-water.
This lotion has to be made fresh every time it is used. It does not do to apply it even the next day, as it will have turned sour. Plantain-water is equally to be recommended.
'Spring, river, and rain water seem to me the first and best of all cosmetics, excellent for every skin. The rather oily juices of melon and of cucumber suit dry skins. Strawberry-juice is good for greasy skins. An infusion of lavender or of marjoram will give tone to a soft skin.'

Face Powder – home-made face powder … Take a new earthenware pot and fill it with six quarts of water and 2½ lbs. of rice; leave the rice to soak for twenty-four hours, and then pour the water off. Put the same quantity of water over the rice for three days running. After the three immersions, each lasting twenty-four hours, drain the rice over a new hair-sieve kept for the purpose. Expose it to the air in a safe place, on a clean white cloth. As soon as it is dry, pound it quite fine with a pestle in a very clean marble mortar with a cover. Then strain it through a fine white cloth placed carefully over the pot which is to hold it, and which ought to be provided with a tight-fitting cover. This powder is better without perfume.
If you run short of home-made powder, you can replace it safely by oatmeal-flour, of which you must take very little at a time on your puff. If you buy your rice-powder, be careful not to choose it perfumed with orris-root, should your skin be inclined to be irritable.
You should never leave your puffs lying about; they should be kept in separate clean china boxes.

Hair Dye – for those women who will not reconcile themselves to wearing their own grey or white hair. Very strong tea dyes light hair which is becoming grey a tolerably good light chestnut. Chicory, in a brown and oily paste, is also a dye for light hair. It should be prepared in a strong decoction. Iron nails steeped in tea for fifteen days will make another dark dye. The dyes of which the base is lead or silver are extremely dangerous. Not only do they bring on baldness but they bring on mischief in brain and eyesight.

Victorian Advice

The section is based on *The Lady's Dressing Room Part III, by Baroness Staff, trans. Lady Colin Campbell, 1893.*

Obesity
A stout woman should not wear a tailor-made dress. It marks the outline too decidedly, and throws every pound of flesh into relief. She must deny herself bows and rosettes of ribbon at the waist, both back and front, as this adornment adds to its size. She ought not to wear short sleeves, as the upper part of her arm is sure to be too fat and look like a ham. A ruffle round the throat will not suit her, nor a very high and tight collar. She ought to have her dress slightly open in a point in the front, or her collar a little turned back. A feather boa is the only one which will not shorten her neck too much. Short basques will make her look ridiculously stout.

Wearing the hair low down will not be becoming to her. She ought to dress it high up on her head, without dragging it too tight; the front should not be plastered down. A certain carelessness in arranging her hair will be best for her, and she must not oil it too much. Patterns with large flowers, or large or small checks, must be avoided for her mantles and dresses. Stripes and plain materials, or small patterns in one colour, are all that she can allow herself and she should wear dark shades.

Few jewels, no pearls round her throat, no earrings, and only as many rings as are indispensable. Sleeves high on the shoulder and with tight cuffs must also be avoided, and she should not wear tight gloves.

Thinness
An angular form and a want of flesh that displays the skeleton under the skin are considered a disgrace in a woman, more especially as a bad complexion nearly always goes with them. It requires courage to listen to the fun people make of a thin woman. Excessive thinness is sometimes joined to an unpleasant temper – a fact mentioned because it is curable. People of this temperament torment themselves; they are busybodies, plaguing themselves and everybody else; they are excitable, impatient, always fussing about. All feminine grace disappears in such an existence.

Fuss is not activity; but a well-ordered activity is advantageous to beauty, to health, to a wisely-regulated life. A thin woman generally has a muddy complexion, because she is often-vulgarly, but truly, speaking-making bad blood. It is her own fault if she does not become pink and white, and rounded in form.

Looking Young
If you wish to keep always young, you must be amiable. A serene face, a sweet expression, a kind and gentle look: these are like a day in spring, and the smile on the lips is a ray of sunshine. Discontented people, always look ten years older than they are. The face gets wrinkled by frowning, pouting causes the mouth to protrude disagreeably, and they rapidly grow old and ugly. Compare with them a woman with a cheerful face; all her features are in their right place, her mouth curves delightfully, benevolence softens the expression of her eyes, and goodness beams from her smooth brow. She is perhaps older than the ill-tempered woman whom you see beside her, but she will always look like her younger sister.

Growing Old Gracefully

It is alleged that women of a certain age do well to practise gymnastic exercises. But this would be very unbecoming to them. If they want to use their arms, why should they not do household work, as was lately prescribed to a northern queen, who followed this sensible medical advice? With the hands protected by gloves, one can dust, brush, and sweep to one's heart's content. This is a sufficient and useful form of gymnastics, natural and healthy, and not ridiculous, like the former.

There is no doubt that the body should be exercised and the limbs kept active. But, above all, we should be cheerful, or at least serene. As we advance in life, let us try to improve ourselves more and more, and to be kind and tolerant. A benevolent disposition and a certain calmness of mind are among the indispensable conditions for preserving good-looks. In mature age, let us put away all pretensions to juvenility. A dowager in a *décolleté* tulle dress, with nothing on her head, is hideous, almost odious. It is her part to wear heavy and rich materials; she should cover her head with a lace mantilla, and her thin shoulders should be draped. A grandmother dressed like her granddaughter, or even like her daughter, is a horrible sight.

She should still, however, continue to love youth in others, to welcome it with pleasure, and to smile upon it. In short, it is stupid to be afraid of the coming years, and which will come all the same. Let us accept our age. An octogenarian who continues to take care of her person can still be beautiful, charming, beloved by her children and her friends, young and old.

The secret of vanquishing old age is not to be afraid of it, nor to shrink from facing the advancing years.

It is, not to resort to absurd, stupid, and dangerous tricks, in the vain hope of retarding it.

It is, to give up a youthful attire, which only makes people look older when it does not suit them.

It is, to keep a kind heart for the young, to like them without being jealous of them.

It is, to retire from the struggle with dignity, not trying to rival your daughters.

It is, to surround oneself with true and gentle affection, which keep the heart green.

It is, to keep up our interest in the questions of the day; to take a delight in talking of great discoveries, of beautiful inventions; not to deny the progress of things, and not to try to make out that the old times were better than the new.

It is, to give advice with gentleness, and not to imagine that years have taught you everything.

It is, to be good and beneficent, in heart and word and deed.

It is, to take more pains than ever with your person. If you neglect any of the little habits of neatness, decrepitude will come on all the faster; and an old person who is careless and untidy presents a far more repulsive appearance than a young one, though such negligence is to be reprehended at all ages.

Finally, it is to wear handsome dresses, rich but simple, without pretension, comfortable, but not necessarily without grace.

Be assured that under these circumstances men and women may overcome old age, and be a pleasure to look at and to be with to the last.

Victorian Etiquette

The information in this section is taken from http://myparlour.stormpages.com/etiquette.htm.

For Young Ladies

Upon being introduced to a gentleman, a lady will never offer her hand. She should bow politely and say 'I am happy to make your acquaintance' or words to that effect.

When bowing on the street, it is appropriate to incline the head gracefully, but not the body.

When travelling by train, tramcar or omnibus, the well-bred lady had a delicate sense of self respect that keeps her from contact with her neighbour, as far as such contact is avoidable.

A lady never looks back after anyone in the street, or turns to stare at them in the theatre, concert hall, church or opera.

A lady never, ever smokes.

In crossing the street, a lady raises her dress a little above the ankle, holding together the folds of her gown and drawing them toward the right. Raising the dress with both hands exposes too much ankle, and is most vulgar.

A lady (or gentleman for that matter) will always rise to their feet in respect for an older person, or one of a higher social standing.

Above all, the lady strives to be dignified and elegant in everything she does.

For Gentlemen

A gentleman will always tip his hat to greet a lady.

When walking in the street, the gentleman always walks on the outside to protect his lady from the dangers of the road.

If a gentleman is smoking and a lady passes by, he should remove the cigar from his mouth.

A true gentleman should always rise when a lady enters or leaves the room, and remove his hat upon entering a room where ladies are present. He should also precede a lady in ascending the stairs, and follow her in descending them.

A gentleman always stands to shake hands.

During the daytime, a gentleman never offers a lady his arm unless to protect her in a large crowd. In the evening, it is appropriate for her to take his arm.

A gentleman should never place his arm on the back of a chair occupied by a lady.

Did You Know?

Until the eighteenth century there was no unified measurement system? In 1795 France alone had over seven-hundred different units of measure!

Before standardisation measurements could differ from one village or town to another as the length of an inch came from either the width of a man's thumb or the distance from the tip of a man's finger to the first joint.

In medieval England an inch was equivalent to the length of three barleycorns. This archaic unit of measurement still underpins the sizing of British shoes today.

The yard came from the length of a man's arm – from nose to fingertip – and the foot from the size of a man's foot. Can you imagine the confusion – people (and barleycorns) came in all shapes and sizes!

Bibliography

Abhishek, Matheesha, 'Christian Dior, The Magic of Fashion', 1994, via https://www.academia.edu/4447558/Christian_Dior_the_magic_of_fashion

Amphlett, Hilda, *Hats: A History of Fashion in Headwear*, Dover Publications, 2003

Anderson, Ruth Matilda, *Hispanic Costume 1480–1530*, The Hispanic Society of America, 1979

Anonymous, *The Chronicles of Enguerrand De Monstrelet: Containing an Account of the Cruel Civil Wars Between the Houses of Orleans and Burgundy; of the … and of Other Memorable Events That Happen*, Ulan Press, 2011

Arnold, Janet, *Queen Elizabeth's Wardrobe Unlock'd*, W. S. Maney & Sons Ltd, 1988

Ashelford, Jane, *The Art of Dress*, The National Trust, 2009

Ashenburg, Katherine, *Clean: An Unsanitised History of Washing*, Profile Books, 2007

Ashton, John, *Social Life in the Reign of Queen Anne: Taken from original sources*, Adamant Media Corporation, 2004

Asquith, Cynthia, *Remember and be Glad – Memoir*, Charles Scribners's Sons, 1952, accessed via Universal Digital Library – https://archive.org/details/rememberandbegla006266mbp

Barber, Elizabeth, *Women's Work: The First 20,000 Years – Women, Cloth and Society in Early Times*, W. W. Norton & Company, 1996

Bayley, John, *Calendars of the proceedings in chancery, in the reign of Queen Elizabeth …*, Vol. 3, Nabu Press, 2011

Bigelow, Marybelle S., *Fashion in History: Apparel in the Western World*, Burgess Publishing, 1970

Bishop, Morris, *The Middle Ages*, new edn, Houghton Mifflin, 2001

Boucher, Francois, *20,000 Years of Fashion*, Harry N. Abrams Inc., 1967

Burns, E. Jane, *Courtly Love Undressed: Reading Through Clothes in Medieval French Culture*, University of Pennsylvania Press, 2005

Calthrop, Dion Clayton, *English Costume painted and described*, Adam and Charles Black, 1908

Cosgrave, Bronwyn, *The Complete History of Costume and Fashion: From Ancient Egypt to the Present Day*, Checkmark Books, 2000

Cunnington, C. Willett, *Handbook of English Costume in the Nineteenth Century*. Plays Inc., 1971

Dawson, Imogen, *Clothes and Crafts in the Middle Ages*, Gareth Stevens, 2000

Downing, Sarah Jane, *Beauty and Cosmetics, 1550–1950*, Shire Books, 2012

Dulaure, Jacques Antoine, *Pogonologia: Or a Philosophical and Historical Essay on Beards*, 1786

Gardiner, Florence Mary, *The Evolution of Fashion*, The Cotton Press, 1897

Gunn, Fenja, *The Artificial Face*, Trinity Press, 1973

Howell, Geraldine, *Wartime Fashion: From Haute Couture to Homemade, 1939–1945*, Bloomsbury Academic, 2013

Hughs, Leo, *The Drama Patrons – Study of the 18th century London audience*, Kindle edn, University of Texas Press, 2013

Kelly, Francis M., *A Short History of Costume and Armour*, Arco Publishing Company Inc., 1972

Ladnier, Penny, 'Colour Names throughout the Centuries', 1996, via http://www.elizabethan costume.net/lizcolor.html

A Lady of Distinction, *The Mirror of the Graces: Or, the English Lady's Costume. Containing General Instructions for Combining Elegance, Simplicity, and Economy with Fashion in Dress* , B. Crosby, 1811, digitised 2008

Laudermilk, Sharon and Teresa L. Hamlin, *The Regency Companion*, Garland, 1989

Lord, William Barry, *The Corset and the Crinoline: A Book of Modes and Costumes from Remote Periods to the Present Time*, Ward Lock and Tyler, 1868

Lublin, Robert I., *Costuming the Shakesperean Stage*, Ashgate, 2011

MacIver, Percival, *The Fan Book,* Frederick A. Stokes, 1921

Mansfield, Alan and Phillis Cunnington, *Handbook of English Costume in the 20th Century 1900–1950*, Plays Inc., 1973

Marly, Diana, *Fashions for Men, An Illustrated History*, Holmes and Meier, 1989

Montez, Madame Lola (Countess of Landsfeld), *The Arts of beauty; or secrets of a ladies toilet: with hints to Gentlemen on the Art of Fascinating*, Dick & Fitzgerald, 1859

Norris, Herbert, *Tudor Costume and Fashion*, Dover Publications Inc., 1997

Olian, JoAnne, *Victorian and Edwardian Fashions from 'La Mode Illustrée'*, Dover Publications, 1997

Pochna, Marie France, *Christian Dior – The Man Who Made the World Look New*, Little, Brown and Company, 1996

Pritchard, Will, *Outward Appearances: The Female Exterior in Restoration London (Bucknell Studies in Eighteenth-Century Literature and Culture)*, Bucknell University Press, 2007

Robinson, Sir Tony, *The Worst Jobs in History*, unabridged edn, Pan, 2005

Russell, Gillian, *Women, Sociabilty and Theatre in Georgian London,* Cambridge University Press, 2010

Stabile, Susan, *Memory's Daughters: The Material Culture of Remembrance in 18th Century America*, Cornell University Press, 2004

Staff, Baroness, trans. Lady Colin Campbell, *The Lady's Dressing Room Part III*, 1893

Steele, Valerie, *Fifty Years of Fashion: New Look to Now*, Yale University Press, 2000

Styles, John, *The Dress of the People – Everyday fashion in 18th Century England*, Yale University Press, 2008

Tarrant, Naomi, *The Development of Costume*, new edn, Routledge, 1996

Vincent, Susan, *The Anatomy of Fashion: Dressing the Body from the Renaissance to Today,* Berg, 2009

Waugh, Norah, *Corsets and Crinolines*, Routledge/ Theatre Arts Books, 1991

Yarwood, Doreen, *European Costume: 4,000 Years of Fashion*, Bonanza Books, 1982

The author at Sudeley Castle. Gown designed and made by Gina Clarke, Tudor Dreams Historical Costumiers, http://tudordreams.weebly.com/, Facebook, Tudor Dreams Historical Costumier.

Index